Ionel Brătianu

Makers
of the
Modern
World

Ionel Brătianu

Romania
Keith Hitchins

HAUS HISTORIES

First published in Great Britain in 2011 by
Haus Publishing Ltd
70 Cadogan Place
London SW1X 9AH
www.hauspublishing.com

Copyright © Keith Hitchins, 2011

The moral right of the author has been asserted

A CIP catalogue record for this book
is available from the British Library

ISBN 978-1-905791-76-7
eISBN 978-1-907822-18-6

Series design by Susan Buchanan
Typeset in Sabon by MacGuru Ltd
Printed in Dubai by Oriental Press

Contents

Acknowledgements   vii
Introduction   ix

I The Life and the Land   I
1 Beginnings, 1864–1895   3
2 Apprenticeship and Reform, 1895–1914   18
3 Great Powers, Small Powers, 1909–1914   48
4 Neutrality, 1914–1916   65
5 War, 1916–1918   80

II The Paris Peace Conference   105
6 Peace, 1919   107
7 Greater Romania, 1919–1927   133

III The Legacy   151
8 Epilogue   153

Notes   158
Chronology   164
Further Reading   206
Picture Sources   211
Index   213

Acknowledgements

My debt to many colleagues and friends who do research and write on Romanian history is great. None is greater that what I owe to my research assistant and doctoral candidate at the University of Illinois, Ms Pompilia Burcică. Her help has been indispensable in the present enterprise. She read and took notes on a great variety of works and her summaries were models of clear thinking and accuracy. In numerous other ways she spared no effort to further the progress of the book. Ms Jaqueline Mitchell and Professor Alan Sharp gave my original draft a critical reading that greatly improved the text. Ms. Adriana Dumitran of the Romanian National Library in Bucharest made many valuable materials available to me. My friends Professor Vasile Puşcaş of the University of Cluj and Professor Lucian Boia of the University of Bucharest have aided in innumerable ways through their own work on the Romanian phenomenon and our conversations over many years. Professor Corina Teodor of the University of Târgu Mureş generously supplied me with rare publications. The steadfast friendship and professional support of Mr Marcel Popa, Director of the Encyclopaedic Publishing House in Bucharest, has been crucial in my study of Romanian history. I have shared ideas and information with many doctoral candidates at the University of Illinois and learned much from them. Working with Ms Zsuzsánna Magdó, Dr Cristofer Scarboro, and Dr Mihaela Wood has been especially rewarding.

Introduction

Ionel Brătianu[1] was the chief representative of Romania at the Paris Peace Conference. He was there by right because of the positions he held: Prime Minister and head of the party in power at the time, the National Liberal Party.[2] It was fitting also that he be there because of all the political figures of Romania of the day he was the one most responsible for his country's being at the conference table. It was essentially his decision to enter the War on the side of the Allies, and it was his steadfastness of purpose that gained for Romania a place beside the major victors.

In a sense, Paris was the culmination of a grand strategy Brătianu had worked out in the preceding quarter-century to raise the modest Romanian nation-state to a European level of prosperity and civilisation and transform it into Greater Romania encompassing all Romanians. It was his single-minded commitment to these causes combined with his grievances as the head of a small power against the mighty that made him an obstacle, if only a minor one, to the smooth course of peace-making.

The burdens he bore and the goals he aimed to achieve were, he was convinced, in harmony with the general course of Romania's development since the first half of the 19th century. He was not, then, the fearless innovator so much as he was the determined heir of those who had laid the foundations. It was a perspective he himself readily accepted, since the objectives he pursued at Paris did not differ in essentials from those espoused by the Liberal tradition forged by his father and his associates. Both generations were intent on creating an independent national state managed in accordance with the principles of European constitutionalism and market economics. He had no doubt that the nation building which earlier generations had initiated, and which he was determined to continue, was perfectly in keeping with the general course of modern Europe's history. That course since the early 19th century, he was certain, had favoured the ethnic nation at the expense of the multi-national empire. He viewed the matter as someone whose country almost from its medieval beginnings had been afflicted by Empires, Great Powers, none of them friendly, and now he had come to Paris to represent the interests of the ethnic nation, his own. It was not surprising, then, that he resisted the efforts of the major Allies to impose their will on lesser Allies.

Ionel Brătianu, like his father, was at the centre of all the great issues that confronted Romania as it followed the path of modernisation. In domestic affairs he was a consistent reformer who believed an enlightened government led by a political party committed to the welfare of the whole nation had a responsibility to respond creatively to changing economic and social conditions and the evolving mental climate. Two issues, in particular, preoccupied him: agrarian reform and the expansion of the electorate. Without them he was certain that neither economic and social progress nor national solidarity could be achieved. As a result, Romania would be consigned indefinitely to the ranks of underdeveloped countries. By distributing land to peasant smallholders and by introducing universal suffrage he intended to enhance the prosperity of all classes of the population and draw them fully into the political process. He thus struck many of his contemporaries as a radical. In fact the reforms he proposed were not experiments in social engineering, but were meant to make existing political and economic structures more durable.

The status of minorities also required his attention, even though his ideal nation-state could only be Romanian. Thus, before the First World War, there was the 'Jewish Question'; and afterwards, with the acquisition of new territories, the Hungarian and German Questions. His solution over the long term was assimilation rather than separate political or cultural autonomies, but his methods were tempered by his liberalism and his sense of belonging to Europe. He took a different stand when it came to the 'Romanian Question' in Hungary, specifically Transylvania, before the War. Here he opposed assimilation of the Romanians as pursued by successive Hungarian governments and argued in favour of cultural and political autonomy for Romanians, since his ultimate goal was their incorporation into Greater Romania, a solution he pursued relentlessly at Paris.

In foreign relations, underlying all his initiatives was a determination to find a secure place for Romania in the European international order. This design, in turn, led him into the heart of the long-standing dilemma that several generations of Romanian intellectuals and political leaders had had to confront: Where precisely in Europe did the Romanians belong? Was their place in the East, because of their traditional Orthodox religion and culture and agrarian, peasant economy and way of life, all predominant before the 19th century; or was their rightful place in the West, because of their country's Roman-Latin heritage and its persistent assimilation of the European style in economic and social life and its integration into the European world of ideas, all in progress since the first half of the 19th century? In the great debate that absorbed the upper layers of Romanian society about the conflicting merits of tradition and innovation, Brătianu placed himself on the side of innovation. He could not conceive of Romania's attaining the goals he had set for it unless the process of Europeanisation continued and a harmonious relationship with the Western powers was sustained. Yet, he was forever wary of the West's embrace, lest it overwhelm the sense of being that ensured Romania's distinctiveness and independence. That, in essence, was his dilemma at Paris.

Ionel Brătianu was an engineer by training, a politician by vocation and a historian by avocation. These occupations complemented one another. His studies of mathematics and structures impressed upon him the value of discipline and facts. The give-and-take of politics taught him how to achieve his ends by combining discipline and facts with the art of negotiation. His avid reading of history allowed him perspective in judging men and events and rendered comfort in moments of trial by reinforcing his sense of destiny to be fulfilled.

As his vision and his realism suggest, he was a Liberal because Liberalism accorded with the spirit of the times and thus made progress certain. Beginning with his observations and experience in his father's house before he entered politics and then during his own career, he never hesitated to adjust the principles and practices of Romanian Liberalism to fit the changing temper of the time. He was a pragmatist, not an ideologue. He was also a nationalist in the sense that the Romanian national state encompassing all Romanians was the supreme ideal which gave meaning to all his endeavours. As a student of European history he had absorbed the lessons of European nation-building in the 19th century. Yet, the sources of his own national feeling lay not in books; it had its roots close to the land, in the rural gentry from which his family sprang; a heritage, however great a moderniser he became, that he never renounced. It was this unique combination of Liberalism and nationalism that governed his behaviour at Paris.

A portrait photograph of the young politician Ionel Brătianu.

I

The Life and the Land

1

Beginnings, 1864–1895

Ionel Brătianu was born on 20 August 1864 on the family estate of Florica, in the *judeţ* (county) of Argeş, some 100 kilometres west of Bucharest, the capital of Romania. The third child and the first son of his parents, he would become heir to one of the great political families of modern Romania, a circumstance that largely determined the course of his life and his choice of career. The countryside and the land remained a powerful influence in both his personal and public life; and however deeply engaged he became in the building of a modern urban and industrial Romania, he would never abandon his rural heritage.

He was descended from generations of mainly small country boiers, a kind of gentry in the 19th century, who possessed significant properties and rose to prominence as local administrators, but who did not seek appointments at the princely court in Bucharest, the capital of the principality of Wallachia until its union with Moldavia in 1859 when a united Romania came into being. Neither did they mingle with the Greek and Hellenised aristocrats, who beginning in the 17th century came in growing numbers from Constantinople and elsewhere in the Orthodox East to Bucharest to make their fortunes, and who as the so-called Phanariot regime were to dominate the political and social life of Wallachia (and of the neighbouring principality of Moldavia) in the 18th and early 19th century.

Ionel Brătianu could trace his family history through the female line back to the 15th century to the Vlădescu family, boiers native to the Argeş region. On the male side the lineage is somewhat obscure for the earlier centuries, but by the end of the 18th century Iane Brătianu, great-grandfather of Ionel, was şătrar, a minor boier rank. His father had married into a prominent boier family of the region, the Vlădescus of Pietroşani and Bucov, who had risen to high office before the installation of the Phanariot regime and counted among their members Şerban Vlădescu, who had served as the Prince of Wallachia's envoy to Vienna in 1688. In this way the Brătianus linked themselves to the old boier families of Wallachia of the 15th and 16th centuries.

Ionel Brătianu's more immediate ancestors were prominent figures in the economic and political life of Argeş. His grandfather, Costandin (Dincă), was not only the wealthiest of all the boiers of Argeş, he was also a person of considerable political influence who became the county administrator (ocârmuitor de judeţ) and represented Argeş in the General Assembly of Wallachia.

Ion C Brătianu, the father of Ionel, was born in the family home in Piteşti on 2 June 1821. He is rightly considered one of the principal creators of modern Romania. By the time his eldest son was born in 1864 he had already left his mark on a series of crucial events that brought about the union of the two principalities and assured the new country's virtual independence. He enjoyed much political influence and was the leading figure among the so-called Radical Liberals. Though a moderniser committed to industry and urbanisation and the Western European model of development, he preserved his ties to the land.

A decisive event in drawing the Romanian principalities closer to Europe was the revolt against the Phanariot-Ottoman regime in Wallachia in 1821. Although the Sultan's army suppressed it, Ottoman rule had been weakened and the Phanariots were replaced by native princes in both Wallachia and Moldavia. Even more decisive in undermining Ottoman predominance was the Russian victory over the Ottomans in their war of 1828–9. By the Treaty of Adrianople of 1829 which ended hostilities, the Ottomans gave up their long-held commercial advantages in the principalities, thereby opening them to international trade. The Treaty also required the Ottomans to pay Russia an immense war indemnity, and until that time it stipulated that Russian troops should occupy the principalities. Between 1829 and 1834, while the occupation lasted, Russian authorities, with the cooperation of the boiers, carried out a reorganisation of the principalities' political and financial institutions that introduced them to the principles of modern administration.[1]

Russian predominance in the principalities ran counter to the growing mood of national self-assertiveness, which stirred the younger generation of boiers, reform-minded intellectuals and middle-class entrepreneurs. A striking display of this new sense of ethnic solidarity was the change of attitude toward folklore on the part of the educated classes, which now came to be regarded with a new sympathy and appreciation for the creativity and way of life of the village. They discerned in rural society the crucial preserver of the essence of the nation in its purest form.

Mihail Kogălniceanu (1817–91), historian, journalist and politician, played a leading role in those events that brought a united, independent Romania into being. As a young man he devoted himself to the study of Romanian history in the belief that knowledge of the past was the surest guarantee of national self-determination. He published *Histoire de la Valachie, de la Moldavie et des Valaques Transdanubiens* in 1837 as an affirmation of the essential unity of all Romanians. A leading proponent of Liberalism in Moldavia, he promoted liberal reforms as the editor of the political and cultural weekly, *Propăşirea* (Progress), and as a participant in the revolution of 1848 in Moldavia. Throughout his career he advocated the awarding of civil and political rights and the extension of cultural opportunities, including schooling, to all citizens, the granting of land to peasants and the emancipation of the Gypsies. Again using his editorship of a newspaper, *Steaua Dunării* (The Star of the Danube, 1855–60), he strove to keep these issues before the public. As Prime Minister under Alexandru Cuza (1863–5), he led the effort to enact reform legislation; and as Minister of Foreign Affairs (1876, 1877–8), he contributed significantly to the achievement of Romania's independence. In retirement he served as President of the Romanian Academy.

At the same time, a 'new history' evolved which focused attention not just on rulers and the mighty but on the whole people, as written by Mihail Kogălniceanu in his *Histoire de la Valachie, de la Moldavie et des Valaques Transdanubiens* (Berlin, 1837). Kogălniceanu and his fellow historians were militant promoters of nationhood, recalling inspirational periods of glory such as the reign of Prince Michael the Brave, who had briefly united Wallachia, Moldavia and Transylvania under his rule in 1600. Their craft, then, could never be an exercise of detached scholarship; its purpose was to foster national unity and promote independence.

Ion Brătianu's early life was typical of young men of his class at a time when the Romanian principalities were opening rapidly to European influence and when French culture and learning were pervasive. He began his education at home with French and Greek tutors and then his father sent him to the local public school in Piteşti. Later, during his stay in Paris between 1841 and 1848, he was attracted to law and political science; and he eagerly involved himself in the activities of young French radicals. He was drawn in particular to the lectures of the liberal historians Jules Michelet and Edgar Quinet and the Polish Romantic poet Adam Mickiewicz at the Collège de France, who urged their listeners to view existing society critically and prepare themselves to change it radically. The effect on Brătianu was to turn him toward liberal democracy, even republicanism; and he joined a group of students led by the radical writer Paul Bataillard, who had founded a review for students at the Collège de France, *Journal des Écoles*, which had as its editor the socialist Louis Blanc.[2]

It was a heady time for young Romanian liberals in Paris. When revolution broke out there in February 1848, and a month later in Wallachia as part of the general European movement to replace the old regime with a liberal order, Brătianu hastened home. In Bucharest he took a leading role in defying the Ottoman suzerain, and with other radicals of similar backgrounds and ambitions he helped to establish an independent Wallachian government in June. Their proclamation, in which they set forth the high principles they bound themselves to follow, was a characteristic document of 1848 in Europe with its emphasis on individual political and civil rights, its advocacy of an increased role for citizens in government and its commitment to good institutions as the instruments of social progress.

The reaction was not long in coming. The liberal experiment was undone in September when Russian and Ottoman troops occupied the country. Both principalities came under a

Russian-Ottoman condominium, which 'supervised' political life in order to discourage any manifestations of the liberal and national spirit that the two powers associated with revolution. The Crimean War, which broke out between Russia and Turkey in 1853 and involved Great Britain and France on the side of Turkey the following year, opened the way for a favourable resolution of the two great issues that preoccupied Brătianu and his fellow radicals – the union and independence of the principalities.

Brătianu had fled into exile in France in 1848, and he remained there until the proclamation of a general amnesty in 1857. In Bucharest again he quickly became one of the leaders of the movement to unite the two principalities, an objective the Romanians themselves accomplished, despite the objections of the Great Powers, by electing the same man as Prince in both principalities in 1859. The new ruler, Alexandru Cuza (1820–73), a boier and a reformer, did much to strengthen the union administratively and to further the cause of full independence, combining the two legislatures and the two armies and making Bucharest the capital of the new 'Romania' as the United Principalities were now officially known.

In spite of Cuza's accomplishments, Brătianu, now the acknowledged leader of the radical liberals, and his colleagues were profoundly dissatisfied with the course Cuza had taken, objecting in particular to his authoritarian tendencies, especially his habit of ignoring the legislature, that is, themselves. They also thought him incapable of assuring the stability and, hence, the security that the new state desperately needed. Convinced that the consolidation of the state within the European system could occur only if it were headed by a foreign prince, they formed a coalition with conservatives that forced Cuza to abdicate in February 1866.[3]

Of the various candidates the conspirators considered, Karl von Hohenzollern-Sigmaringen of the Catholic branch of the Prussian Hohenzollerns was Brătianu's choice and it was he who accompanied him to Bucharest on May 8. Two days later the Constituent Assembly formally proclaimed Carol (Karl) their Prince, and in October he secured recognition from his suzerain, the Ottoman Sultan, as ruler of a state 'united in perpetuity'. The Constituent Assembly had already promulgated a new constitution in July, a document based in large measure on Western experience, which provided solid legal foundations for the development of a modern state over the next half-century. It was a clear reflection of the optimism and the aspirations of the rising liberal middle class, whose leaders Brătianu and his fellow radicals were intent on becoming.

Brătianu served as Prime Minister continuously from 1876 to 1888, except for a few months in 1881, and as a political force he was second only to Carol. For all these years he benefited from a congenial working relationship with Carol, which was based on their agreement in principle on crucial issues of domestic and foreign policy. Brătianu recognised Carol's primacy in foreign policy, especially his reliance on Germany, and agreed to his initiatives in military affairs such as his reorganisation of the Romanian army in accordance with the Prussian model. Carol, in turn, allowed his Prime Minister relative freedom in domestic affairs as long as he respected the prerogatives of the Crown and did not tamper with the prevailing structure of society.

During Brătianu's long tenure the contours of modern Romania took form. In international relations he led the long struggle for independence to a successful conclusion by allying Romania with victorious Russia in war against the

Ottoman Empire in 1877 and by deftly manoeuvring at the Congress of Berlin in 1878 to gain the sanction of the Great Powers for independence. But he suffered disappointments, too, at Berlin, as Russia required Romania to cede the southern districts of Bessarabia taken from it after the Crimean War, despite earlier promises to respect Romania's territorial integrity. The episode could only reinforce the Romanians' mistrust of Russia. Brătianu proceeded to champion the proclamation of Romania as a kingdom in 1881 to enhance the country's international standing and concluded a pact with the Triple Alliance of Germany, Austria-Hungary and Italy in 1883 to provide security for the new kingdom, especially against Russia. In domestic affairs he created a strong bond between the Liberal Party and the rising industrial and banking middle class. He mobilised these forces skilfully to transform the economic foundations of the country from agrarian and rural to industrial and urban. By using the powers of the state to the utmost, he was determined to bring about the modernisation of the Romanian economy and society as the prerequisite for security, prosperity and a high level of civilisation.

It was in this atmosphere of liberal challenges to tradition and of dynamic nation building and, no less, of political rivalries and gamesmanship that Ionel Brătianu spent his childhood and adolescence. His was a family that prized hard work and personal achievement; and it recognised service to the nation as the ultimate satisfaction to be gained from all these endeavours. Until the age of 14 he grew up mainly in the rural setting of Florica, a small estate that his father had bought in 1858 and had so named in memory of a daughter who died in infancy. Located in the rolling countryside some 15 kilometres east of Piteşti, it offered the young boy an idyllic existence and was to serve the later statesman as an indispensable refuge from the travails of politics in Bucharest. He remained attached to Florica all his life, despite the family's move to Bucharest in 1878 to assure the children a better education than that available in Piteşti and to accommodate the more intensive work schedule of Ion Brătianu, who had become Prime Minister on 24 July 1876.

The education Ionel Brătianu received had public service as its underlying theme. Despite the constant press of politics and the complexities of government administration, Ion Brătianu devoted much time to the education of his children, going even into the smallest details in order to instil in them respect for productive labour and a sense of patriotic duty. At a time when families of his class were sending their sons and daughters to Europe for an education, he insisted that his own have a Romanian education in order to strengthen their attachment to their country. He therefore enrolled Ionel in the National College of Saint Sava in Bucharest, the leading secondary school in Wallachia. Ionel displayed a particular aptitude for mathematics, which may have influenced his and, more important, his father's choice of career for him. In any case, his father was adamantly opposed to his becoming a lawyer, because, he complained, it was lawyers more than anyone else who had caused him so much grief in Parliament. He settled on engineering because he was persuaded that it would both give his son the opportunity to cultivate his skill in mathematics and further the modernisation of the country.

After graduating from Saint Sava in 1882, Ionel did six months obligatory military service in the artillery corps. Then, in the autumn of 1883, his father sent him, well prepared in mathematics and French, to the Lycée Sainte-Barbe in Paris where he soon discovered to his dismay that his training at home had left him ill-prepared for the rigors of French secondary education; but he persevered and earned good grades.[4] He seems to have developed no close friendships, a pattern that had also characterised his teenage years at home, where his closest friend was his sister Sabina.

His training to become an engineer began in earnest in 1884, when he passed the entrance exams to the Polytechnic School in Paris and was admitted; and it continued when in 1886 he began taking courses at the School of Bridges and Highways. These studies, at which he worked very hard, rekindled his long-held interest in mathematics and persuaded him to pursue a doctorate in the subject. He planned, first of all, to take his license at the Sorbonne, but to his great disappointment he failed the entrance exam.

He seems to have made few friends among his French fellow students, preferring, instead, the company of Romanians; but he by no means sought to isolate himself from the society around him and he warmed to the varied social and cultural opportunities that came his way. Friends of his father from the era of 1848, such as Paul Bataillard and his family, welcomed him regularly into their home and introduced him to their friends and acquaintances. Nonetheless, his most sustained and enjoyable relationships were with Romanian families who had taken to living for extended periods in Paris. He thus moved in high Romanian society, receiving invitations from Ion Ghica, a leading political figure and influential writer on economic matters, and from Alexandru Odobescu, a pioneering archaeologist and writer of short stories and secretary of the Romanian legation in Paris (1881–5). He also became a constant and welcome presence in the household of Vasile Alecsandri, a leading poet and playwright.

During this time he also went regularly to the theatre and

attended important cultural events, such as the reception of the poet Lecomte de Lisle, the leader of the Parnassians, into the French Academy in 1887. He seems to have made it a point to keep abreast of intellectual and cultural trends in Paris as a faithful reader of the daily press and of the well-known fortnightly journal of literature and the arts, the *Revue des Deux Mondes* of Paris. He also added to his impressive store of historical knowledge whenever he could. Once, on leaving one of his classes at the Sorbonne, he stepped into a nearby amphitheatre to hear a 'most interesting' lecture on Frederick William I of Prussia, who had transformed his realm into a powerful and efficient state in the early 18th century, by the young, influential historian Ernest Lavisse.[5]

Brătianu was a keen observer of the differences of mentality and spirit that distinguished Western Europe from his own part of the continent. After a visit to the Church of St Sulpice on Christmas Eve 1887, he came away praising the music of the mass as 'beautiful' and the interior of the church as 'magnificent', but he confessed that he preferred the Romanian Orthodox service as more intimate, even though it was also more 'barbarian'. At St Sulpice he thought the priests were too detached from the congregation, reading the service only for themselves and using a language (Latin) unknown to the majority of the faithful. It all seemed to him a little theatrical with the bells and the movements of the priests suggesting a ballet, a performance inappropriate in a church.[6]

Throughout his six years in Paris his professional training came first. He was intent on learning as much as possible about the numerous branches of engineering so he could choose the career that, as he wrote to his father in a letter of June 1888, would be of greatest use to his country when the time came. But he could not decide between industrial and hydraulic engineering. To help him make up his mind he visited the workshops of the Paris-to-Lyon rail line and asked his father's close friend and 'grey eminence' of the Liberal Party, the banker Eugeniu Carada, for a letter of introduction to Gustave Eiffel, the already famous engineer who in 1889 was to build the tower that bears his name, to enable him to visit his workshops. On another occasion he took a cruise on the Seine with Anghel Saligny, a leading Romanian engineer in the service of the state-run Romanian rail system, to see how the bridges spanning the river had been constructed. He also toured the Parisian sewer system, which impressed him with its complex organisation and the efficient manner in which waste water was treated.

During his stay in Paris he had the opportunity to travel extensively in Western Europe. In the spring of 1886 he visited England. He observed everything and everybody, noting how often during the day the English ate, how their servants were 'first-rate' and how English boys and even girls were taken with sports and how cricket, lawn-tennis and football were played everywhere.[7] He was thoroughly enchanted with London, finding it ... *the queen of cities, not only in size [...], but also in its beauties, which I found in no way inferior to Paris.*[8]

Eugeniu Carada (1836–1910), economist, journalist and politician, has often been described as the 'gray eminence' of the Liberal Party and, in any case, was one of the leaders of the Brătianu wing of the party, the so-called 'Occult'. He played a key role in the establishment in 1880 of the National Bank of Romania, which became one of the power bases of the Liberal Party and a crucial instrument it used to carry out its economic policy. He was a confidant of both Ion C Brătianu and his son, and used his considerable influence to have Ionel elected president of the party in 1908 succeeding Dimitrie A Sturdza. He never held a ministerial post and was never elected to Parliament, but was often entrusted by Liberal governments with important financial missions.

In the summer of 1888 professional interests took Brătianu to north-western France to inspect all types of engineering and industrial enterprises and then on to Belgium, especially to see the great port of Antwerp. In the Flemish region he was struck particularly by the constant struggle the inhabitants waged with nature, by the enormous effort they had to put forth in order to perform the 'miracle' of transforming sandy, barren soil into rich, productive farmland through irrigation.

From the very beginning of his stay in Paris he had kept a close watch on the ups and downs of political life at home. He was well acquainted with the principal political figures in both of the major parties, Liberal and Conservative, and was an unrelenting critic of the Conservative opposition. In the spring of 1889 he took his final exams and was awarded his engineering degree. Eager to apply what he had learned, he returned home. He had no desire to remain longer in Paris, whose way of life had always seemed alien to him.

The Romania to which he returned was well on its way to becoming a modern state. The population was increasing (from roughly four and a half million in 1877 to nearly six million in 1899) and was slowly becoming more urban. Industrialisation, however uneven, was making significant progress, bolstered by an expanding infrastructure of everything from railroads to banks. Economic development and the expansion of the civil administration and public services led to significant changes in class structures, with the rise of the middle class (its upper ranks in the first instance) to a position of not only economic but also political pre-eminence. Yet, in many respects the characteristics of underdevelopment remained everywhere apparent. Agriculture continued to be the foundation of the economy as the overwhelming majority of the population lived in the countryside and depended mainly on

agriculture for its livelihood. As for its organisation and production methods, agriculture had progressed but little since
the middle of the century. Although industry was develop-
ing apace, the widespread poverty of the rural areas meant
there was little local market for goods. Abroad, Romania was
steadily being drawn into more complex commercial and
financial connections with Western and Central Europe, but
the relationship was hardly a partnership of equals: rather,
the country was increasingly reliant on foreign manufacturers
of goods for both the consumer market and industry, and on
foreign investments to spur economic growth.[9]

Ionel Brătianu was deeply troubled by what seemed to
him the willingness of many Romanians to yield the levers of
economic power to others. But for now he embarked upon a
career in engineering at the urging of his father, who advised
him to place himself at the service of the state without getting
involved in politics: first, he should prove himself as a professional and only afterwards consider a career in public life.
Accordingly, in the autumn of 1889 at age 25 he entered the
service of Anghel Saligny, who was now in charge of building and maintaining bridges for the state-run Romanian rail
system and had recently been commissioned to design a steel
bridge to span the Danube at Cernavoda, which when com-
pleted in 1895 would be the longest such bridge in Europe.
Saligny put Brătianu to work inspecting old railway bridges
along the Danube River and choosing those that needed to be
replaced. As Saligny's confidence in his young assistant grew
he assigned him more demanding tasks, notably the construction of railway lines in Moldavia in 1891. He also engaged his
services for the construction of the Danube bridge.

Yet, however faithfully Ionel Brătianu performed his duties,
the pull of politics was irresistible. In a letter of April 1890

to his brother Dinu in Paris listing his favourite occupations, he put politics first before bridges and even the vineyards at Florica. After his father's death in 1891 he yielded to family tradition and pressure from prominent Liberal Party leaders, in the first instance, Eugeniu Carada and Dimitrie Sturdza, the head of the party, and abandoned his budding engineering career for politics.

In 1895 he stood as the Liberal Party candidate for Gorj County, just to the west of Argeş. He was a vigorous campaigner who was anxious to raise fundamental issues of economic development and education with his audiences, but he was not a dynamic orator capable of stirring enthusiasm in his listeners. Rather than indulging in dramatic pronouncements and exaggerated promises (the 'pompous rhetoric' he criticised as one of the chief ills of contemporary politics), he went directly to the heart of things, even complex issues, and gradually and painstakingly enlightened his audiences as to the causes of problems and his own solutions. In any case, his election was all but certain since Dimitrie Sturdza had already received the call from the King to form a government and thus, in accordance with custom, took charge of 'organising' the elections. Brătianu's victory was the first of many, as he would never suffer a personal defeat at the polls. Politics henceforth became his life, and Bucharest was the arena in which he pursued his ambitions.

2

Apprenticeship and Reform, 1895–1914

After his election and entrance into the lower house of Parliament, the Chamber of Deputies, Ionel Brătianu rose rapidly within the Liberal Party hierarchy. His ascension was marked by appointments to posts in every Liberal government between 1895 and 1909, when he became Prime Minister. He had the continuous support of the so-called 'Occult', a small, influential group of Liberals headed by Eugeniu Carada, now Governor of the National Bank of Romania, the largest financial institution in the country. Carada and his colleagues operated out of the public view, 'in the shadows' as a critic put it. They saw in Ionel Brătianu a young man of enormous political talent with whom they planned to gain control of the party and set it and the country on a vigorous course of reform and modernisation.

Brătianu's first cabinet position was Minister of Public Works in 1897 at the age of 33. It was followed by appointments as Minister of Public Works again in 1901, Minister of Foreign Affairs in 1902 and Minister of the Interior in 1907. From the beginning he acknowledged the obvious: how much he owed to his famous name. At a banquet of party faithful in April 1897 he told the story of a young officer on horseback carrying the national flag at a military ceremony and how when he passed by the row of generals they drew their swords and saluted. Only a fool, Brătianu reminded his audience, would think they were saluting the young officer; they were saluting the flag as the symbol of national unity. *I know that the name I bear is my chief title*, he conceded, *but I do not regret the fact; I take it as a powerful incentive to do my duty and emulate those who have preceded me.*[1]

'I know that the name I bear is my chief title, but I do not regret the fact; I take it as a powerful incentive to do my duty and emulate those who have preceded me.'

IONEL BRĂTIANU, APRIL 1897

Brătianu and the Liberals came to power five times between 1895 and 1908, as the so-called rotation system with the Conservative Party worked with relative smoothness. According to the unwritten rules of Romanian politics, the two major parties – the Conservatives and Liberals – alternated in forming governments at more or less regular intervals after Ion C Brătianu's resignation in 1888. Both parties were committed to maintaining the constitutional monarchy and the existing political and social order as defined in the Constitution of 1866, but there were significant differences in their approaches to contemporary issues and their overall idea of how Romania should develop. The Conservatives generally represented the interests of the large-landowning class, whereas the Liberals championed the aspirations of the burgeoning commercial and industrial middle class. Although a blurring of the boundaries between classes accelerated in the latter decades of the 19th century, the large land-holders (and that class of intermediaries between them and the peasants who worked their estates – the leaseholders or *arendaşi*), by and large favoured free trade since it enabled them to export their grain and cattle to world markets at competitive prices, whereas the business and industrial classes sought protective tariffs and other forms of state intervention to shelter their still modest enterprises.

Only a small number of citizens participated directly in political life. Income requirements, the system of electoral colleges and indirect voting, and government manipulation severely limited access to the electoral process and thus reserved the power of decision to the possessing classes. The revised Constitution of 1884 created three electoral colleges, the first two representing the well-off of the countryside and of cities and towns who elected 145 members of the Chamber of Deputies, and the third representing the peasants who could elect only 38 deputies. The number of eligible voters in 1905 for each college was 15,973, 34,742, and 42,907, respectively, for a total of 93,622 out of a population of nearly six million. The number of electors for the Senate, who were divided into two colleges, was even smaller: 10,659 and 13,912, respectively, 24,571 all together. The parliamentary elections of 1911 reveal clearly that the well-to-do in both rural and urban areas, that is, the large landowners and the commercial, industrial and banking upper bourgeoisie, dominated political life. In that year 73,633 voters chose the Chamber of Deputies and 18,003 the Senate.[2]

A further crucial influence on the outcome of elections, and hence on the functioning of the political system, was exerted by the King through his constitutional power to appoint the Prime Minister. In the final three decades of Carol's reign (1866–1914) the procedure for changing governments achieved a high degree of refinement. It began with consultations between the King and leading political figures over the choice of one of the latter to form a government to take the place of the one that had just resigned. The newly designated Prime Minister then chose his Cabinet and proceeded with the organisation of elections for a new Parliament. In this process the Minister of the Interior bore a heavy responsibility, since it was he who directed the considerable bureaucratic apparatus at the centre and at the local level throughout the country to take all necessary measures to ensure the sitting government's electoral victory. Thus, between 1881 and 1914, no Prime Minister so designated by the King ever failed at the polls. Yet, despite these limitations on democratic government, the political system assured extensive civil liberties to individual citizens, including freedom of association and assembly and the widest possible freedom of the press. All these guarantees help to explain the often agitated, impassioned nature of political life at the time.

There was no place in this rotation system for third parties of any ideological persuasion, though there were several attempts to create parties that would represent citizens other than the great landowners and the upper bourgeoisie. These included Take Ionescu's Democratic-Conservative Party. It was mainly the party of lawyers and other professionals and of small and middle-size landowners. It had more the attributes of a faction than an independent party and never fully separated itself from one or another of the main currents in the Conservative Party. On behalf of the peasant majority the Peasant Committee (*Comitet Țărănesc*) founded a separate political party to champion their interests. Led by Constantin Dobrescu-Argeș, a young schoolteacher from Brătianu's home county, it was formed of so-called village intellectuals, mainly schoolteachers, better-off peasants and some clergy and artisans, and became a formal party, the Peasant Party (*Partida Ţărănească*) in 1895. It sought comprehensive agrarian reform, but neither it nor its successor, the new Peasant Party (*Partidul Ţărănesc*) founded in 1906, became a significant force in political life. The small but growing urban working class was represented by the Social Democrat Party of Workers of Romania (*Partidul Social-Democrat al Muncitorilor din România*), founded in 1893 by mainly middle-class intellectuals who advocated a gradualist approach to economic and social change. Faced by a persistent failure at the polls, the majority of its leaders decided in 1899 to join forces with the Liberal Party as the best means of advancing the cause of socialism in the foreseeable future. It was not until 1910 that more radical Socialists succeeded in creating a cohesive party, the Social Democratic Party of Romania (*Partidul Social Democrat din România*), reaffirming its revolutionary character. But it remained on the margins of political life.

Brătianu and the Liberals were, on the whole, the beneficiaries of the prevailing political system; and Brătianu himself did not immediately challenge it. Satisfied for the time being to work within the framework of the old order, he proved to be an effective manager of the several Ministries he presided over. He soon became well-known for his command of facts even down to the smallest details and for the energetic way in which he put his ideas into practice. Characteristic of his approach was his reorganisation as Minister of Public Works in 1897 of the way grain was exported. He overcame the shortage of railway wagons used in exporting grain by building new repair workshops. But he was also intent on finding ways to diversify methods of sales and exports, *as they do in the United States*.[3] Ever the politician, he also understood how

Take Ionescu (1858–1922) was trained as a lawyer, but made politics his life's work. He began his political career as a Liberal and then switched to the Conservative Party in 1886. Within a short time he became a leading figure in Romanian politics, noted for his oratorical gifts and served in numerous Conservative governments. As Minister of Cults and Public Instruction (1891–5), he initiated numerous reforms in the education system and provided the Romanians of Transylvania with subventions for schools and churches from the state budget. A person of strong opinions, he preferred to lead rather than follow and thus he founded his own party, the Democratic-Conservative Party in 1908. His individualism may explain why he was Prime Minister only once, and then only for a month at the end of 1921 and the beginning of 1922. He was an advocate of agrarian and electoral reforms and worked with Brătianu and the Liberals to enact the necessary legislation in opposition to the Conservatives. During the First World War he was a staunch advocate of Romania's entering the conflict on the side of the Entente as a means of uniting all Romanians in a national state, and after the defeats suffered by Romanian armies in 1916 he joined Brătianu in a national unity government. During the Peace Conference in 1919 he worked tirelessly in Paris and London on behalf of the Romanian cause, even though he had no official position. He favoured cooperation and conciliation with the Allies in order to achieve Romania's aims rather than the tactic of confrontation employed by Brătianu. After the War, as Minister of Foreign Affairs (1920–1), he took the lead in creating the Little Entente of Czechoslovakia, Yugoslavia and Romania as a means of preserving the Versailles settlement.

to profit from his official functions, and he was thus rarely absent from public ceremonies celebrating his successes.

The higher purpose of his involvement in politics, as he saw it, was to bring Romania fully into the modern world at a European level of civilisation and economic prosperity. He recognised the special importance of the political party as the indispensable instrument with which he could achieve his goals. But if it was to accomplish its mission, it must enforce discipline and unity of purpose within its own ranks. The

Liberal Party was to be Brătianu's instrument for achieving great things for the country, but he and younger Liberals were dissatisfied with the course their party had taken since the retirement of his father in 1888, and especially with Dimitrie Sturdza, who had been its president since 1892.

Dimitrie A Sturdza (1833–1914), Liberal politician and historian, returned home from studies in Germany in 1857 and immediately entered politics, spending nearly his entire life in that profession. He was a Minister in numerous governments between 1866 and 1908, President of the Liberal Party from 1892 to 1908, and Prime Minister four times between 1895 and 1908. A moderate and a representative of the so-called old Liberal tradition, he was often at odds with Ionel Brătianu and his younger colleagues. He also pursued a scholarly career. During his long tenure as Secretary of the Romanian Academy he placed it on a solid financial foundation and greatly enriched its collections of documents with purchases and his own donations. He himself edited numerous collections of sources on the history of the Romanians.

Sturdza belonged to an older generation that retained strong links to the countryside and its traditions of political thought and action and was thus wary of rapid change. The moderation practised by Sturdza and his supporters seemed to Brătianu ill-suited for dealing with the critical economic and political issues of the day, specifically, national underdevelopment, widespread poverty and the exclusion of the majority of citizens from public affairs. He was eager to bring the party back to the kind of radicalism his father had stood for in 1848 and as Prime Minister and to make it once again the 'motor of change'.

In his determination to reinvigorate the party he welcomed newcomers and displayed a remarkable breadth of views as he attempted to keep the Liberal Party from becoming the representative of a single social class, a turn he thought would prevent it from carrying out its national mission. The nature of Brătianu's party-building and the range of his political ideas are revealed in the warm reception he accorded the former leaders of the Romanian Social-Democratic Party in 1899. These so-called *generoşi* (the generous) had come to the realisation that economic and social conditions in Romania had not matured sufficiently to make a Socialist movement viable and had thus decided that they could best serve their cause by joining the Liberal Party. They had been attracted particularly by Brătianu's forward-looking brand of Liberalism and his oft-stated intention to press forward with fundamental economic and political reforms, all of which they thought would strengthen bourgeois democracy and capitalism, thereby creating the necessary conditions for the transition to Socialism. For his part, Brătianu appreciated the commitment of these moderate Socialists to solving the grave problems that impeded the country's modernisation. He also discerned in them valuable allies in wresting control of the Liberal Party from the Sturdza Liberals and turning it into a force for innovation and progress.

As Brătianu's political career advanced, he gradually brought stability to his private life. He enjoyed the company of women, and they found him attractive, but it is difficult to escape the sense that his romantic relationships and, later, family obligations were always secondary to politics. His correspondence reveals almost nothing about his emotional attachments. Yet, unlike his father's generation and even his own, he did not think it obligatory to contract matrimonial alliances with Liberal families. Rather, he chose his lover and first wife Maria Moruzi and his second wife Elisa Ştirbey from high Conservative society. Princess Maria Moruzi, whom he met at the beginning of his engineering career, was the widow of one of the sons of Prince Alexandru Cuza, the first modern ruler of united Romania. Out of their union a son,

Maria Alexandra Victoria of Saxe-Coburg (1875–1938), Queen of Romania, was born in Eastwell Park, a manor house near Ashford in Kent, England. She was the daughter of Alfred, Duke of Edinburgh and son of Queen Victoria, and of Maria Alexandrova, daughter of Tsar Alexander II of Russia. She married Ferdinand von Hohenzollern, nephew of King Carol I of Romania and heir to the Romanian throne, in 1892 and became Queen of Romania when her husband ascended the throne on the death of Carol I in 1914. She identified herself completely with her adopted country and became enormously popular with the public because of her personal charm and her charitable work during the First World War with wounded Romanian soldiers and with civilians who had also become casualties of war. She was a staunch supporter of the Entente and worked subtly to bring about Romania's entry into the War against the Central Powers. After her son Carol II came to the throne in 1930 and undertook to marginalise members of the royal family, she largely withdrew from public life. She was the author of numerous collections of stories and novels, many of which were inspired by Romanian sources. Especially important are her memoir, *The Story of My Life*, 2 Vols (New York, 1934–5), covering her life up to 1918 and her 'Daily Notes' (1918–38), both of which provide an intimate view of Romanian society and politics.

Gheorghe, was born in 1898 before their marriage, who was to become one of Romania's leading historians and an influential Liberal Party politician in his own right in the inter-war period. His parents did marry, but each lived a separate life. They were soon divorced, and Brătianu did not see his son until much later, in 1909. He had numerous opportunities for marriage after the divorce, and shortly after the turn of the century he became romantically involved with Paulina Astor of the wealthy and prominent Astor family of New York. She was in the circle of friends around Marie, wife of Prince Ferdinand, heir to the throne.

Marie and Brătianu were to cross paths on numerous occasions, and, though they were of quite different temperaments, they never failed to cooperate when the best interests of the country were at stake. Marie formed a generally favourable opinion of Brătianu early in their relationship, around 1900, while he was a young government Minister. In essentials it remained unchanged. She found him to be good company, 'pleasantly ironical', but always on guard and determined that nothing should escape his attention. She appreciated his witty and always stimulating conversation, and she recognised behind this congenial exterior an 'unyielding personality conscious of who he was and what he represented for Romania'.[4]

Brătianu achieved the desired order in his private life with his marriage to Elisa Ştirbey in 1907. The daughter of Prince Alexandru Barbu Ştirbey, an important Conservative political figure and the son of Prince Barbu Ştirbey, ruler of the Principality of Wallachia in the early 1850s, and the former wife of the Conservative Party leader Alexandru Marghiloman, she was noted in Bucharest society for her sharp intelligence, high culture and fluent French and, much rarer at the time, English. She was a faithful supporter of her husband's political career and became his confidante, one of the few people he fully trusted. Thus, only to her would he give for copying the texts of the treaties of alliance that bound Romania to enter the First World War on the side of the Entente in August 1916. They had no children.

> 'Burdened with the glory of his father, Ion Brătianu was, however, a personality even without his name, and what was more important to me then, Ion Brătianu was an eminently agreeable companion and, let it be added, Brătianu II was a lady's man.'
>
> **MARIE, QUEEN OF ROMANIA,** *THE STORY OF MY LIFE,* **VOL 1 (NEW YORK, 1934), PP 422–3**

For Brătianu his mission in life – to raise Romania to the level of the advanced nations of Europe and to bring all

Romanians together in a national state – superseded all other concerns. At the centre of his grand design was the modernisation of the economy, a task, he was certain, that could be pursued successfully only within a broad European framework. As an engineer engaged in constructing a modern rail network, then as Minister of Public Works in 1897 and Minister of Foreign Affairs in 1902, and as an amateur historian he had become convinced of the need to cooperate closely with the acknowledged masters of international commerce and banking. He looked to the West for investments and technical expertise and could not conceive of Romania's making significant progress if it were forced to rely solely on its own resources. Yet he was equally determined to protect national interests. The nature of the international financial and economic system, dominated as it was by the great industrialised states, made him anxious. He judged the operation of the prevailing order to be nothing other than a competition between the powerful and the weak that amounted, in effect, to an economic war. The Western European powers were pursuing it with *an intelligence and extreme perseverance* that offered no quarter to anyone. He cited the Americans, the *most powerful and dangerous competitors* Romania faced in the oil business, as typical of the modern economic spirit, and he warned that anyone familiar with the organisation and temperament of the American oil trust could have no doubt that its goal was absolute domination of the oil trade.[5] And so, he reasoned, Romania had continually to be on guard as it entered more deeply into this *uncertain world*.

Brătianu's concerns about how Romania should develop and about the proper relationship it should have with the West were shared by the majority of Romanian politicians, economists, writers and social thinkers in the latter decades of the 19th century and the beginning of the 20th. In a sense, they were all engaged in a great debate about who the Romanians were as a nation and what path of development was best suited to their nature and would thus lead them most surely to material prosperity and a high level of civilisation. The diversity of opinion on these vital issues was enormous, but two general tendencies stood out. One recognised the debt Romania owed to Western Europe's experience and thus could see no other path for the country to follow than industrialisation and urbanisation. The other drew inspiration from Romania's deep-rooted agricultural and peasant heritage and, as a consequence, set itself against the radical changes promised by 'Europeanisation' in favour of traditional social and economic organisation and the spiritual values it nurtured.

The beginning of the modern debate about identity and paths of development may be dated from the activities of the Junimea (Youth) Society of Iași in the 1860s, which aimed to stir debate among Romanians about who they were and where they belonged in Europe. Titu Maiorescu, who was to become a leading figure in intellectual life and education for almost half a century and was Prime Minister on the eve of the First World War, was their chief spokesman. Young 'Westernisers' in their eagerness to hasten the modernisation of their country, he lamented, had borrowed wholesale the cultural and political forms of the West, which were, after all, the products of an urban, middle-class society, and had unthinkingly forced them upon a society that was overwhelmingly rural and peasant and thus ill-suited to receive them. The Junimists proposed a return to the 'organic sources' of Romania's long evolution and the cultivation of traditional moral and spiritual values. They had no doubt that Romania would evolve toward a modern civilisation like that of Western Europe, but these changes could be only in a moral and cultural sense because they could not foresee a time when agriculture would lose its predominant place in economic and social life.

Titu Maiorescu (1840–1917), philosopher, literary critic and politician, took a leading role in creating a modern, 'authentic' Romanian culture. Besides his efforts to keep borrowings from European culture within the bounds of Romanian social realities, he insisted on the importance of aesthetics in judging works of literature. A man of wide interests, he became engaged in all the great controversies of the time over Romanian literature, language and historical development. A major figure in the Junimist wing of the Conservative Party, he served as a Minister in numerous Conservative governments, becoming Prime Minister, 1912–14.

The Sămănătorists (Sowers), led by the historian Nicolae Iorga, held a similar view of Romania's development and were especially vehement in their denunciation of capitalism as destructive of the 'authentic way' of life and customs of the Romanian countryside. Their remedy was not social and economic reform but rather a moral renaissance brought about gradually through the dissemination of a healthy culture. At the heart of their theory of social development, then, was the certainty that change, to be beneficial and lasting, must be evolutionary.[6] The Populists, who shared with the Sowers assumptions about the fundamental agrarian nature of Romanian society and the need to eliminate the 'deviations' of the 19th century and return to the authentic sources of organic development, were intent on improving the conditions of life for the mass of the population through extensive economic and social reforms. They also differed from the Sowers through their insistence that Romania was a part of Europe and had much to learn from Europe's experience.[7]

On the other side of the great debate were the Europeanists, characterised in the ideas of the economist Petre S Aurelian (1833–1909), a staunch advocate of industrialisation and
protectionism and a prominent Liberal. Early in his career he
had espoused free trade, but later came to the conclusion that
Romania, by pursuing an open-door policy, was in danger of
becoming a kind of colony of the advanced industrial and
financial powers through *modern means of conquest* and
thus could never hope to be master of its own destiny. Romania's only salvation, he urged, was to take the same path of
development as they – industrialisation.[8]

Brătianu felt most at home with the Europeanists, sharing
many of Aurelian's concerns. Like them, he favoured industrialisation and urbanisation and integration into Western
Europe's intellectual and cultural world. He thought all of
this was in the long run inevitable, but he insisted that the
Romanians themselves could not stand by as mere observers
of the process; they must come to grips with key problems
and use their state institutions and their political parties to
remove the barriers to national progress. Of all the issues that
confronted the country, he held agriculture to be the most
urgently in need of attention. In his persistent advocacy of
agrarian reform he deviated somewhat from the characteristic emphasis of his fellow Europeanists on industrialisation.

For Brătianu and for Romanian elites in general the Great
Peasant Uprising of 1907 was a shock and a call to action.
The unprecedented loss of life and destruction of property
brought home to them in ways they had never before experienced the gravity of what for decades had been routinely
referred to as the 'Peasant Question'. The Conservative government proved utterly incapable of dealing with the crisis
and at the end of March 1907 was replaced by the Liberals,

who proceeded to suppress the Uprising with the use of the army under the command of General Alexandru Averescu. Brătianu as Minister of the Interior had primary responsibility for restoring order in the countryside and revealed fully his abilities as a planner and organiser as he dealt firmly and prudently with the most severe internal crisis the country had faced since Carol's accession in 1866. By the middle of April a relative calm had been restored, but the cost in lives and property had been enormous.

The uprising of the peasants brought home to Brătianu (and to many others of the elite) the magnitude of the crisis facing the country, which he feared would threaten its very survival if left unattended. Over a decade before the uprising, at the very beginning of his political career, he had put the problems of agriculture high on his agenda and he had been eager to impress upon influential groups the urgent need for change. During his first electoral campaign for a seat in Parliament in 1895 he had boldly linked the country's future to the welfare of the peasantry, raising questions about whether a democratic state could endure unless a sense of solidarity prevailed that would allow each person to contribute his share to the achievement of society's common aspirations.[9] Once elected, he had kept agriculture and the peasant constantly before his fellow deputies in parliament.

He knew very well, however, that the peasant question was not simply an economic matter. It was, for him, also a matter of education – how, he wondered in a parliamentary speech in 1905, could the peasant improve his condition if he could not read or write, and he reminded his listeners that Romania had one of the highest illiteracy rates in Europe – and of understanding the rural mentality and way of life. He stressed the need to channel a greater portion of the education budget into the building and improvement of rural schools and the establishment of more teacher-training colleges.

In the aftermath of the peasant uprising Brătianu became ever more forceful in his advocacy of immediate, far-reaching changes to the traditional organisation and practices of agriculture. He was one of the few politicians who treated the problems of agriculture as an integral part of the country's overall economic development. He pointed out that in normal circumstances, that is in Western and Central Europe, agriculture, industry, commerce and cities complemented one another, but Romania deviated sharply from the European model. How, he asked, could industry and commerce prosper in a country that was overwhelmingly peasant and in which the peasant consumed so little? How could agriculture be improved without sustained industrialisation and urbanisation? Who should take the lead in setting matters right?

Brătianu was for bold action on a wide front. Crucial, he thought, would be changes in the relations between landholders and peasants. He was particularly harsh in his criticism of large-scale lease-holding, whose dire effects, he pointed out, the 1907 uprising had made plain. He was critical of large property in general because its holders had forgotten that property was a social institution. He admitted that they indeed had rights, but he also insisted that property imposed obligations on the possessors toward all those whose livelihoods depended on its productivity and proper management.[10] As the landholding system had evolved over several centuries it had ceased to be for peasants a means of making a living, but had instead, he complained, created *a link of misery between the peasant and the land*. He repeatedly pointed to the need of peasants for proper schooling to enable them to take advantage of new ways of cultivating their plots and thereby increase their incomes. No less pressing, he thought, was the extension of credit to the peasants on reasonable terms especially to smallholders, and he had only praise for the modest local banks (*băncile populare*) that were actively engaged in meeting peasant needs.

The essential issue that lay behind all Brătianu's thinking on agriculture was the role of the state as the only body capable of taking the bold action necessary to place agriculture on a new, solid foundation. The state, through the Parliament, then, would enact the required legislation and would create the means of monitoring compliance with the new laws. He proposed that a Higher Council of Agriculture and a corps of agricultural inspectors be created for the purpose. Together they would reconcile the conflicting interests of landowners and peasants in order to increase labour efficiency, improve the quality of the grains produced and expand exports, and in this way raise the standard of living of all concerned.

He had long been persuaded that effective reform would require a lifting of the prohibition in the Constitution against expropriating private property for the public good because he recognised the small size of the majority of peasant holdings as one of the main causes of the agrarian problem. He claimed repeatedly to be fully committed to the principle of private property, but he also pointed to the overriding interest of the state in fostering social harmony and promoting the general welfare. If the disparity between large properties and smallholdings was putting the public interest and the security of the state at risk, then he thought it imperative that land from large estates be expropriated in order to provide the most deserving peasants with plots sufficient to allow them not only to survive but to prosper. In a speech in Parliament on 26 November 1907 he cited Otto von Bismarck's justification for expropriation. In 1886 the German Chancellor had pointed out that no one thought it extraordinary that the state could expropriate hundreds of kilometres of land for a railroad or a whole quarter of a city to build a port. Why then, he asked, couldn't the state exercise its powers of expropriation to prevent an uprising? Wasn't the peace and security of citizens just as important as the transport of goods?[11] Such reasoning reflected Brătianu's own approach. He declared his readiness to undertake the difficult, to some the revolutionary, task of amending that section of the Constitution that declared private property inviolable.

In promoting modernisation, Brătianu was faithful to his liberal economic heritage. He recognised the compelling need for Romania to build up its industries, if it were to become a modern state and take its rightful place in Europe. He conceived of industrialisation as part of a broad strategy of development in which industry, agriculture, international trade, enlightened credit and education would complement one another. Aware that Romania lacked the material and human resources essential to the success of his ambitious enterprise, he was prepared to rely on the financial and technological assistance of Western Europe. Yet, even as the country drew more and more on foreign expertise and investments and reaped the benefits, he was troubled by the dangers that such borrowings posed to national economic independence. He thus adamantly opposed granting foreign companies a monopoly over entire branches of the economy and its infrastructure. When the Conservative government of Petre Carp was inclined to grant far-reaching concessions to foreign firms in order to weather a severe financial crisis in 1900, Brătianu raised a cry of alarm in Parliament about surrendering to *our economic adversaries*, citing the efforts of the American corporation Standard Oil to gain a dominant stake in the Romanian oil industry as the type of *cooperation* to be avoided at all costs.[12]

His thinking about foreign investments was guided also by his general view of international economic (and political) relations. They represented, he warned, a contest between the haves and the have-nots, between the powerful industrialised states and the weak agricultural countries. Who in such a competitive climate, he wondered, would look after Romania's interests, if the Romanians themselves failed to do so?[13] In a 1900 article in the Liberal Party daily, *Voinţa Naţională* (The National Will) he complained that too many politicians were ready to ignore the national interest in return for short-term financial advantages. Yet while he warned against the pitfalls of free trade and the unfettered flow of capital into Romania from abroad, he recognised the impossibility of economic growth if the country were to take refuge in some form of autarky. It should be evident to everyone, he thought, that Romania for some time to come would have to import capital and technology and even skilled workers in order to accomplish its national goals. Yet, it should also be just as clear that Romania was a player, though a modest one, in the international economic system and had something of value to contribute. In any case, he argued, Romanians could not sit on the sidelines; they had to take the initiative to gain a share of the world's trade and wealth. They also had to expand their horizons to grasp the fact that what happened in New York and Chicago was more important for the Romanian businessman in Bucharest than what happened in Craiova, a commercial centre to the west.

Brătianu's long wait to put his modernisation projects into motion ended in the final days of 1908 and the beginning of

1909. Dimitrie Sturdza, long in declining health, informed the King on 27 December that he could no longer bear the burdens of leadership and resigned. The Occult and other prominent Liberals unanimously chose Brătianu as his successor as party leader because, as one of them put it, he combined talent, hard work, youthful vigour, experience and a name that symbolised the best traditions of the Liberal Party. He was duly summoned by Carol to form a new government. At the age of 45 he had become head of the most powerful political instrument in the country and could now concentrate on bringing his bold plans for economic progress and prosperity and, no less, a measure of social justice to fruition.

As head of the Liberal Party and as Prime Minister Ionel Brătianu was at last in a position to shape policy and initiate direct action in keeping with his vision of what the Romania of the future should be. His first term as Prime Minister lasted two years, from January 1909 to January 1911. For most of this time he was also Minister of Foreign Affairs and Minister of the Interior, a typical accumulation of powers intended to discourage rivals within the party. His grand design was to blur the line that separated East from West by turning Romania into an economically advanced, modern state. He never wavered in his commitment to this ideal, either in office or in opposition. The tenacity he had honed as a boy and a

'My husband liked him, but his liking was tinged with a slight feeling of diffidence as though unsure on what ground he was treading. There was something a little overpowering about Brătianu which awoke an uneasy sensation; his glove was of velvet but one was not very sure what lay beneath.'

MARIE, QUEEN OF ROMANIA, *THE STORY OF MY LIFE*, VOL 1 (NEW YORK, 1934), PP 422–3 young man at school and in the shadow of his father proved crucial now, as the tasks he faced were daunting and the characteristic rough-and-tumble of Romanian politics showed no signs of abating.

The Romania over which he now presided had moved toward modern social and economic forms by the turn of the century. The population was slowly becoming more urban, industrialisation was making evident progress and the infrastructure was steadily expanding. Yet, underdevelopment persisted. Agriculture had undergone little innovation in structure and level of productivity, and those who were mainly responsible for both organisation and production – the peasants, still nearly 80 per cent of the population – were not sharing adequately in the general progress of society. The majority remained poor, illiterate, ill-nourished and ill-housed. Industry had indeed grown, but key branches, such as metallurgy and machine-building, were still unable to satisfy domestic needs, and there was continued economic dependence on foreign investments and manufactured goods.

Romania's Europeanisation was also reflected in its literature with signs of innovation evident in the literary language which was becoming more supple and expressive, in the emergence of new genres, notably the novel, and in the predominance of new currents such as realism and symbolism. Writers also turned increasingly to the urban world for complex, artistically challenging themes. Among them, the dramatist and short story writer Ion Luca Caragiale (1852–1912) infused Romanian literature with the spirit of the city as he depicted the constant restlessness, dissatisfaction and pursuit of minor triumphs of the lesser bourgeoisie of Bucharest. In modern Romanian literature's first cycle of novels following the fortunes of an old boier family, Duiliu Zamfirescu

(1858–1922) helped lay the foundations of the Romanian realist novel and strove to urbanise and intellectualise, in short to Europeanise, the Romanian novel. In poetry the champion of symbolism, Alexandru Macedonski (1854–1920), superbly represented the spirit of innovation and experiment in theme and form that characterised the best work of the time and endowed Romanian poetry with new sounds and original means of expression.

Ionel Brătianu pressed ahead with reform on a broad front, despite the lack of adequate resources and the formidable opposition to structural change from the King, the Conservatives and even important figures in his own party. He remained convinced throughout his career that modernisation could not proceed unless outmoded agrarian structures were reformed and the negligence of the material and cultural needs of the majority of citizens and their virtual exclusion from public life were ended. He turned for guidance and even at times for consolation to Romanian and European history of which he was an avid reader. He was continually adding to his formidable library and archive at Florica. Of all the subjects that attracted his notice, the striving of the peoples of Europe to achieve national unity and independence was foremost. He drew inspiration especially from the ideas and writings of leading figures of the German and Italian unification movements of the 19th century, and he frequently held them up as examples for the Romanians to emulate as they pursued their own national aspirations. But he thought that the Romanians' own past should serve as an inspiration, too.

From history he knew that national unity and social and economic progress could not be achieved without struggle, that the Romanians could not be absent from the conference tables or the battlefields of Europe when great decisions were being made about the continent's future and that the Romanians must not fail to find a secure place for themselves within the European state system. He often remembered how his father, both before and after he became Prime Minister, had insisted that Romanians take part in every international conference or conflict that affected their region. Even in 1853, well before the two principalities had been united, he wanted their princes to join the Allied side in the Crimean War, if only with a single regiment of troops, on the grounds that whatever would be decided at the peace conference without the Romanians would be decided against them. Persistent struggle and stark realism were his son's watchwords, too. Thus, Ionel Brătianu reasoned that Prussia had succeeded in uniting Germany and had transformed it into a powerful empire not through peaceful demonstrations of brotherhood with other German states, but by excluding a rival, Austria, from the German Confederation.[14]

Of all the creators of new European states in the 19th century, Brătianu most admired Camillo di Cavour, the Piedmontese statesman who had taken skilful advantage of currents and rivalries in the international relations of the time to bring about the unification of Italy. He hoped to emulate this in Romania. He praised Cavour for his audacity, for pressing forward with the *great work* of Italian unification at a time when such a goal appeared revolutionary or even quixotic and contrary to the interests of Europe. But Brătianu judged Cavour's *construction of Italy* to be, in fact, *conservative* and wholly in keeping with the *inexorable course* of modern Europe's history, which, to his mind, was nation-building.[15] For the Romanians he discovered a similar audacity and momentary defiance of Europe in the actions of his father and his fellow radicals who had pressed forward with the union of Moldavia and Wallachia in 1859, even though most of Europe was against it. The Romanians then and later, he argued, were the creators of their own destiny; but, like Cavour, they understood that if their success was to be lasting, they must impress upon Europe their value to the international system. In particular, he wanted to offer a strong, united Romania to the Great Powers as their primary guarantor of peace and stability in South-eastern Europe.

Brătianu's main goals were economic and political modernisation and the consolidation of a Romanian national state within the framework of European civilisation and with the approval of the Great Powers. To accomplish his ends he intended to mobilise *national forces*, by which he meant all the moral, intellectual and material resources the country could provide. No part of the population was to be left out of the common effort to create a more prosperous society and a stronger state. When one of his long-time rivals, Take Ionescu, an orator and parliamentarian of exceptional skills and the leader of the Democratic-Conservative Party, accused him in a speech in 1911 of ignoring the interests of the middle class because of his preoccupation with the peasant question, Brătianu responded by reminding Ionescu that a healthy bourgeoisie could hardly exist in a country where the great majority of the population lived in poverty.[16]

His thought about development was guided by a body of ideas known as 'Neo-Liberalism'. The general outlines of the doctrine as applied in Romania had become clear well before the First World War, its reach being all-inclusive, covering the political and economic system, social structures and international relations. For Brătianu and many of his younger colleagues, various aspects of traditional Liberalism had become outmoded; they no longer corresponded to the needs of a young nation like Romania striving to become modern as rapidly as possible. He feared that the political system with its limited franchise which largely excluded the peasantry and growing urban working class was in danger of alienating the majority from the elites and from the state itself.

The 'Liberal Manifesto' of 1911, which he largely formulated, was suffused with the Neo-Liberal principles and practices of the time and gave priority to the economy. It advocated rapid industrialisation and the creation of a truly Romanian industry and an end to reliance on agriculture as the main source of national wealth and well-being. Brătianu's conception of Neo-Liberalism required a balance between the power of the state to make economic interventions and respect for private property rights. In political and social terms Brătianu understood the new Liberalism to have as its primary goal national solidarity, that is, the re-establishment of a harmonious relationship between the mass of the population and the leading classes. He proposed to restore social harmony in two ways: first, by drawing the masses into public affairs through the abolition of the three electoral colleges in favour of one, a change that would eliminate indirect voting and make all citizens genuine participants in the political process; and, second, by apportioning land more equitably, a reform that would allow the peasant majority to share at last in the benefits of economic progress.

Out of office in 1911, Brătianu nonetheless continued to refine his vision of the new Romania. The agrarian problem remained at the centre of his ambitions. On 20 September 1913 Brătianu published in *Viitorul* (The Future), the official newspaper of the Liberal Party, a comprehensive plan centred on large-scale land reform and universal suffrage. He knew the implementation of both measures would require forceful

Petre Carp (1837–1919) was a leading Conservative almost from the beginning of his political career. His university education, like that of many of his fellow Conservatives, was German. Along with Titu Maiorescu, he was one of the founders of the Junimea Society in Iaşi in 1863, and he adhered faithfully to the Junimist brand of conservatism, which combined an admiration for European culture with a critical sense of economic and social realities at home that discouraged radical experiments. He was a Minister in numerous governments and performed a variety of vital services for his country. He helped to arrange a meeting between Otto von Bismarck and Prime Minister Ion C Brătianu which led to Romania's joining the Triple Alliance in 1883; and he dealt skilfully with serious economic and financial problems in the 1890s. One of the leading theoreticians of Romanian Conservatism, he was president of the Conservative Party (1907–12) and served as Prime Minister twice (1900–01 and 1910–12). At the outbreak of the First World War in 1914 he championed Romania's immediate involvement on the side of Germany, and in 1916 he passionately opposed Ionel Brătianu's decision to join the Entente against Germany and with Russia.

intervention by the state, and he now used the fateful word 'expropriation' for the first time in public, which for many, even in his own party, had revolutionary connotations. At the party congress two weeks later on 2 November he declared his intention to seek necessary amendments to the Constitution to enable the state to seize private property and to create a single electoral college.

The opposition to his project was immediate and widespread. The Conservatives would have none of it. Petre Carp announced he could accept expropriation of land only if large industrial enterprises and the National Bank (institutions where the Liberals held sway) were nationalised. He thought it unjust to single out for sacrifice just one social class, the large landowners, who had contributed so substantially to the welfare of the country. Even more moderate

Conservatives would give Brătianu no quarter. Titu Maiorescu and Alexandru Marghiloman declared expropriation
a 'revolutionary and anarchic' method of dealing with society's problems and unworthy of a party of order and stability.
King Carol was also opposed, as he was to every measure he
thought threatened existing social and political structures. He
made his sentiments clear by refusing to accept a government
of national union led by the Liberal Party in place of Maiorescu's Conservatives.[17]

Brătianu needed a united Liberal Party behind him but
his bold project had caused deep unease among many of the
Liberal faithful who thought he had fallen under the spell
of the Socialists. To counter this he took his case for reform
directly to the membership in a series of public meetings in
the autumn of 1913 in which he denied that the party was
abandoning its support of private property. Quite the contrary, he argued; by granting land to the peasants, the party
would, in fact, be strengthening respect for private property
by increasing dramatically the number of those attached to
the land. The long-term result of agrarian reform, he insisted,
would be to consolidate existing political and social institutions by drawing the mass of the population into public life
and thus encouraging them to accept the ideal of the national
state as represented by the Liberal Party.[18] Party leaders closed
ranks and Brătianu persuaded Carol to accept the proposed
reforms by agreeing that they be carried out with moderation
and that he would reach an understanding with the Conservatives on how to amend the Constitution with a minimum of
public wrangling. Carol clearly had confidence that Brătianu
could bring controversial matters to the desired conclusion.

At the same time Brătianu was pushing hard for agrarian
and electoral reform he had to deal with an equally delicate

matter – the so-called Jewish Question. Shortly after he became Prime Minister for the second time, he received a letter dated 7 February 1914 from the former Prime Minister of Italy, Luigi Luzzatti, protesting against the treatment of Jews in Romania. It was signed by, among others, Georges Clemenceau (a member of the French Senate, leading exponent of democracy and stout defender of Alfred Dreyfus, the Jewish officer in the French army wrongly accused of selling secrets to Germany) and David Lloyd George (a leader of the Liberal Party in the British Parliament and Chancellor of the Exchequer).

The issue Luzzatti raised had become increasingly serious in Romania in the latter part of the 19th century. As the Jewish population grew and as Jews took an increasingly important role in business, banking and the professions, political authorities reacted by imposing limitations on their activities. Article 7 of the 1866 Constitution denied citizenship to non-Christians. Both Liberals and Conservatives enforced numerous regulations intended to limit Jewish immigration and settlement, especially in rural areas. Jewish organisations abroad, in particular the Alliance Israélite Universelle in Paris, and sympathetic Western European governments intervened on behalf of Romanian Jews and put pressure on Romanian governments to soften the harsh legislation they had enacted against Jews. At the Congress of Berlin in 1878 the powers demanded that Romania modify Article 7. But in succeeding decades neither the Conservatives nor the Liberals had significantly lightened the civil and social disabilities that weighed on a Jewish community that numbered 240,000 in 1912.

Luzzatti's letter seems to have caught Brătianu off guard. In the aftermath of the Peasant Uprising of 1907 he had thought the Jewish Question purely one of economics, not of race or religion. In 1907 he roundly condemned the lease-holders, most of whom were Jewish, as 'persons of evil intent' who had created an ugly situation; but he was convinced that as agriculture prospered and the condition of the peasantry improved, the Jewish Question would gradually resolve itself. In his long letter of reply to Luzzatti of 22 February 1914 he reiterated his certainty that the matter that concerned them both had nothing to do with religion or race. The Romanians, he insisted, were too tolerant for such attitudes to influence their behaviour, and he cited as proof naturalised Jews who participated in *all areas of Romania's life*.[19]

The general tone of Brătianu's letter, however, was far from defensive. He admitted that much work still had to be done before the great majority of Jews could be integrated into Romanian society, the solution that he himself strongly desired. He pointed to the important, even preponderant, place Jews had attained in commerce, industry, banking and the artisan trades as evidence that Romanian society offered them equality of opportunity. Yet, he could not help voicing the sentiment held by many Romanians that the Jews themselves were partly responsible for the ill-feeling directed against them. They had, Brătianu insisted, emigrated in large numbers to the principalities, especially Moldavia, in the middle of the 19th century and had engaged in selling alcohol and money-lending among a population, peasants mainly, who were still in a *primitive* economic state. Jews, he complained, had taken advantage of their inexperience and had thus contributed greatly to the growing impoverishment of this population and, in doing so, had threatened to *compromise the foundations of the state*.[20]

Brătianu was blunt in telling Luzzatti and the co-signers

of his letter that the Jewish Question was a strictly Roma-nian problem. He thought it in the interest of the Jews them-selves to make certain that it remained a domestic matter. He viewed *with unease* the efforts of international Jewish organisations, in a show of *cosmopolitan solidarity*, to bring pressure to bear on the Romanian state. In thus attempt-ing to internationalise the matter, they had raised questions about Romania's independence and its right to manage its own affairs. His response was the same position his father had taken at the Congress of Berlin in 1878. It was a stance he himself would take at Paris in 1919, when the Allies insisted that Romania sign a Minorities Treaty assuring equal rights of citizenship to Jews.

Brătianu now pressed forward with his reforms. A general understanding within the Liberal Party on agrarian and elec-toral reform and the acquiescence of the King in the need for the expropriation of large land-holdings had cleared the way for his return as head of a Liberal government on 4 January 1914. The Liberal-dominated Parliament duly voted to revise the Constitution and then was dissolved on 22 April to make way for the convocation of a National Constituent Assembly. New elections, which the Liberals won, were held on 18 and 26 May, and on 5 June the Constituent Assembly held its first meeting. On the 21st it chose a commission to draft projects of reform and then adjourned until November, when it would debate and vote on the commission's proposals. The outbreak of the First World War persuaded Brătianu to postpone any further consideration of internal reform in the interests of national solidarity. His attention was now to be absorbed by international events.

3

Great Powers, Small Powers, 1909–1914

Ionel Brătianu knew that Romania occupied only a modest place in an international system dominated by the Great Powers. In a speech in the Senate on 15 May 1913 during a debate on the gathering Balkan crisis he pointed to the obvious: small states simply had no representation in the Concert of Europe. But he was also persuaded that if *the ignored* could find an efficient institutional means of promoting their common interests, then they could become a force in international relations *at least equal to one Great Power.* His contentious advocacy of the rights of small powers was the leitmotiv of his diplomatic initiatives during his first term as Prime Minister and then throughout the First World War and at the Paris Peace Conference.

He saw no necessary contradictions in a foreign policy that put Romania first and at the same time tried to harmonise national objectives with those of the Great Powers. He believed that small or medium-size states could achieve their ambitions in international affairs only in association with one or more of the Great Powers. He never doubted that

Romania's national interests could be served best by an orientation toward the West, rather than eastward or toward the Balkans. Indeed, Central Europe, that is Germany and Austria-Hungary, was for him the arena where Romania's fate would be decided most immediately. He could not, therefore, conceive of Romania's alienation from the West. To secure an enduring place for his country in Europe's consciousness he was determined to pursue an activist policy that would demonstrate its value as a contributor to regional peace and stability. At this point, two issues seemed to him of paramount importance: the maintenance of a balance of power in the Balkans and the improvement of conditions for the Romanians in Transylvania.

At first, as Prime Minister, Brătianu preserved the traditional framework of Romanian foreign policy and did not deviate from the general course it had taken since the War for Independence in 1877–8. Its cornerstone was the Triple Alliance of Germany, Austria-Hungary and Italy, created by treaty between Germany and Austria-Hungary in 1879 and adhered to by Italy in 1882. After Romania achieved independence at the Congress of Berlin in 1878 it sought a firm commitment of support from one or more of the Great Powers, as a guarantee of protection against Russia – the chief threat to its independence.

Romania adhered to the Triple Alliance in 1883 in the form of a bilateral treaty with Austria-Hungary. The two sides promised to come to the aid of the other in case of an attack by Russia (although it was not specifically named), and they agreed not to join any alliance directed against either of them. Germany adhered to the treaty the same day in a separate act. King Carol and Ion Brătianu insisted that the treaty be kept secret because they were certain if it were made known, it would cause a violent reaction from many politicians and the general public who were mainly pro-French. Thus, the alliance with Austria-Hungary and Germany, the bedrock of Romanian foreign policy for nearly three decades, was never submitted to Parliament for ratification. Its maintenance and periodic renewals depended on Carol and a small number of Liberal and Conservative politicians who had to be let in on the secret.

Relations between Romania and Austria-Hungary were never smooth. There was a lack of warmth and trust on both sides, as revealed by the bitter tariff war they engaged in between 1886 and 1893, which in the end harmed the economies of both countries. Even though normal commercial relations were gradually restored and the material damage caused largely repaired, the long-term result of the conflict was to reinforce the underlying hostility that the majority of Romanians felt toward Austria-Hungary. Such a strained atmosphere hindered cooperation in matters of foreign policy and tended to magnify the seriousness of other issues. These included the treatment to which the large Romanian population of Transylvania was subjected by the Hungarian government as it sought to transform multi-ethnic Hungary into a Hungarian national state. King Carol and other proponents of the alliance with the Central Powers became increasingly alarmed as hostility toward Austria-Hungary over the 'nationality question' in Transylvania grew among the public and began to be the subject of heated debates in Parliament. It raised doubts about the strength of Romania's attachment to the Triple Alliance not only in Bucharest but also in Berlin and Vienna. Another source of tension between Romania and Austria-Hungary came to the fore with Bulgaria's declaration of independence in 1908 and evident intention to expand its boundaries at the expense of the Ottoman Empire and create a Greater Bulgaria. King Carol and Brătianu viewed an aggressive and enlarged Bulgaria as a threat to Romania's own aspirations to predominance in the region. They expected their alliance partner to provide full diplomatic support, but Austria-Hungary had other objectives in the Balkans.

Even though Ionel Brătianu's personal sympathies lay with France and Great Britain, he had long recognised the crucial importance of Romania's partnership with the Triple Alliance. It offered the new state protection from aggressive neighbours (in the first instance, Russia), and he judged the support of Germany and Austria-Hungary essential for the success of Romania's ambitions in South-eastern Europe. He had great respect for Germany's military strength, and he had been impressed by the close cooperation between Germany and Austria-Hungary and the rapidity with which the latter had mobilised during the crisis in 1908 over its annexation of Bosnia and Herzegovina.

Yet Brătianu was reluctant to renew the treaty with the Triple Alliance even though the King had made foreign policy his special province and had impressed on Brătianu (and his predecessors) that he would never abandon the alliance with Germany. Brătianu knew the King disliked his own activism in international affairs and his domestic reforms. He also must have realised that the leaders of the Central Powers hardly viewed him as a friend. They much preferred Dimitrie Sturdza as both Prime Minister and head of the Liberal Party because he was a moderate and predictable and had promised never to make fundamental changes in foreign policy without prior consultations in Vienna and Berlin. Brătianu's accession to both posts alarmed them. They regarded him as the head of the 'chauvinist wing' of his party and thus as someone intent on achieving aims that were incompatible with loyalty to the Alliance.[1]

In late July and early August of 1909 Brătianu travelled first to Vienna to meet Austro-Hungarian Foreign Minister Graf Alois Lexa von Aehrenthal and then to Berlin for discussions with German Chancellor Theobald von Bethmann-Hollweg to reassure them of his commitment and to clarify issues of importance to Romania. He used the occasion to reaffirm Romania's obligations to the Alliance, but in Berlin he made it clear that Romania would continue to cultivate the *best possible relations* with the Alliance only as long as Germany was its directing force.

The primary objective of Brătianu's trip was to gain German and Austrian support for his Balkan policy. He was anxious, first of all, to preserve the status quo south of the Danube, a desire he thought fully in accord with the aims of his allies and the Great Powers generally. He wanted his partners to understand that Romania was not a Balkan state, that it did not participate in the unrest and violence that he himself thought endemic to the region. Yet he was equally emphatic that the Balkans were of vital concern to Romania. He called Bethmann-Hollweg's and Aehrenthal's attention to Bulgaria's *inordinate* ambitions, which he feared, if carried to their ultimate ends, would upset the balance of power in Southeastern Europe and do immeasurable harm to Romania's and the Great Powers' interests. He warned that Romania could not remain indifferent to Bulgaria's territorial expansion and that he himself would be hard put to explain to Romanians of all political stripes what advantages the alliance with the Central Powers had brought them, if Germany and Austria-Hungary failed to intervene forcefully on Romania's behalf.[2]

His hosts were hardly reassuring. Bethmann-Hollweg

pledged that Germany would continue to cultivate close relations with Romania, but on the matter of territorial compensation in the Balkans he was non-committal. In Vienna, Brătianu was more blunt; he told Aehrenthal that in case of war between Bulgaria and Turkey, Romania might be obliged to mobilise and occupy a part of Bulgarian Dobrudja. In response, Aehrenthal was not at all sympathetic to Brătianu's threatened intervention, which he politely characterised as 'inconvenient'. He reminded Brătianu that by treaty Austria-Hungary was bound to support Romania if it were attacked, not if it were the attacker. He therefore recommended direct negotiations with Bulgaria and, if those failed, he urged him to wait for the general peace conference to press Romania's claims. He promised that Austria-Hungary and Germany would faithfully represent Romania's interests and fulfil all their treaty obligations.[3]

The second critical issue Brătianu raised in Berlin and Vienna was the status of Romanians in Transylvania. Ever since the 1890s the nationality problem in Transylvania had grown in importance as an obstacle to cooperation between Romania and Austria-Hungary. Brătianu was still persuaded that Balkan problems were for the time being more urgent, but he was anxious to keep the Romanian question in Transylvania on the Central Powers' agenda until the time when it could become a valuable bargaining tool for Romania. Nonetheless, he thought the continued curtailment of the Romanians' right to free political and cultural expression by the Hungarian government would eventually become an insurmountable barrier to normal relations with Austria-Hungary and thereby endanger what mattered most to him: the alliance with Germany. What worried him especially was his perception that Vienna had allowed Hungarian political leaders too strong a voice in determining the Dual Monarchy's foreign policy.

All in all, his conversations with Aehrenthal and Bethmann-Hollweg had been enlightening. He could now gauge more accurately the long-term value of the Alliance for Romania, since in neither Vienna nor Berlin did he encounter more than lukewarm support for the issues that concerned him. He returned home with his earlier resolve to explore new directions in foreign policy strengthened.

After his government had been replaced by the Conservatives in January 1911 Brătianu observed the growing competition between Austria and Russia for influence in the Balkans with unease. He viewed Russia's response to Austria's annexation of Bosnia and Herzegovina – the encouragement of an alliance of Balkan states against Austria – as ominous. Then, as war between the Ottoman Empire and the Balkan allies (Bulgaria, Serbia, Greece and Montenegro) seemed unavoidable in the summer of 1912, Brătianu urged the government to order mobilisation and prepare to intervene. But the King, whose views in foreign policy usually prevailed, preferred to negotiate a settlement of territorial issues in Dobrudja directly with Bulgaria. He was convinced that more could be gained by neutrality than by immediate involvement because he expected a drawn-out conflict which would eventually require the intervention of the Powers to restore peace and order. Romania, by maintaining a peaceful and balanced posture, he reasoned, would be seen as a force for stability in the region and as a reward would be invited to the peace conference as a full participant, thereby giving it pre-eminence over its smaller Balkan neighbours.

The surprisingly easy victories of the Balkan allies in October and early November 1912 came as an unpleasant surprise for the King and the Conservative government. Brătianu repeated his demands for mobilisation and intervention as the surest way of protecting Romania's vital interests in the region, but the government persisted in its policy of neutrality. As the Powers set to work to fashion a solution that would restore the general peace and foster their own interests in the Balkans, relations between Austria-Hungary and Romania steadily deteriorated. Both Liberals and Conservatives and the King became thoroughly exasperated with the Austrian leaders' handling of the complex issues involved, particularly their failure to defend Romania's interests.

The Austrians found themselves in the middle. They tried to satisfy both Romanians and Bulgarians and wound up alienating the Romanians. The chief architect of Austria's policy, Graf Leopold von Berchtold, who had become Foreign Minister in 1912, was eager to bring Bulgaria into the Triple Alliance as a counterweight to Serbia, which had become increasingly hostile to the Dual Monarchy. As a result, rather than supporting Romania's territorial claims on Bulgaria, he sought a peaceful compromise of their differences. But the Romanians interpreted his stand as a reneging of earlier Austrian protestations of support. Thus, when Graf Franz Conrad von Hötzendorf, Chief of the Austrian General Staff, came to Bucharest in November 1912 with promises to represent Romania's interests 'vigorously' neither the King nor the Conservative government was put at ease. Nonetheless, Carol promised Conrad that in the event of a European war Romania would fulfil its obligations to the Alliance. Conrad could thus leave Bucharest reassured that the links to Romania were still firm, but he was clearly worried about the attitude of Ionel Brătianu toward Austria and about the extent of his commitment to the Triple Alliance.

Brătianu himself had been alarmed by the easy victories of the Balkan allies and by what seemed to him the Conservative government's unwillingness to press Romania's claims against Bulgaria forcefully. The intervention of the Great Powers to bring about a general settlement and prevent the crisis from involving the Powers in a confrontation amongst themselves did little to allay his concerns. The negotiations between Romanian and Bulgarian delegations that they sponsored in London in December 1912 and January 1913 proved fruitless. As the Bulgarians persisted in rejecting Romanian proposals for a new boundary line in Dobrudja between Turtucaia and Balchik as a maximum or Silistria and Balchik as a minimum, King Carol threatened military action. Conrad tried to mediate, but he ended by merely confirming Romanian suspicions that he was primarily intent on wooing Bulgaria. While the atmosphere was clouded by these unresolved issues Romania and Austria-Hungary renewed their alliance for another seven years in February 1913. Yet, both sides were aware of how fragile their ties had become, for it would soon be time for the Liberals to replace the Conservatives, and Brătianu had made no secret of his sympathies for the French-British Entente. In the meantime, the continued impasse between Romania and Bulgaria led the Powers to convene a Conference of Ambassadors in St Petersburg, which in May 1913 awarded Romania Silistria and a three-kilometre zone around the city. But this compromise satisfied no one. The Romanians came away aggrieved by what they saw as Austria-Hungary's partiality toward Bulgaria. The estrangement deepened in May and June as the Balkan allies moved toward war among themselves over the division of the territory seized from the Ottomans, notably Macedonia. Berchtold took the occasion to warn the Romanian government to avoid an alliance with Serbia or Greece because such action would be judged unfriendly and contrary to the interests of the Triple Alliance.

A remarkable consensus on what had to be done was now achieved in Bucharest. King Carol, Conservatives and Liberals, far from being intimidated by Berchtold's admonitions, became more determined than ever to pursue an independent policy toward Bulgaria. Brătianu, speaking for the majority of Liberals, urged the King to take vigorous action in order maintain the *Balkan equilibrium*. In particular, he pressed the idea of a mobilisation of reservists in order to serve notice on Bulgaria that it could not expand its territory with impunity.[4] The new, activist mood continued to gain momentum and undermined what links remained to Austria-Hungary still further.

Brătianu now saw Romania confronted with the kind of situation he had been anxious to avoid: the balance of power in South-eastern Europe upset and rival Bulgaria enlarged, all happening with Romania standing on the sidelines. In a debate in the Senate on the conduct of Romanian foreign policy at the end of May, shortly after the provisions of the Treaty of London of 30 May 1913 ending the war had become known, he castigated the Conservative government for its lack of foresight. Rather than pursuing a vigorous foreign policy that would give Romania a voice in decisions affecting its security and welfare, Prime Minister Titu Maiorescu, he charged, had not demanded anything, but had instead waited for others to bring gifts. Such an attitude he characterised as merely *noble poetry [that] had nothing to do with the prose of reality*.[5] A great historical process was continuing to unfold before them, he warned, with the Romanians failing to be properly engaged.

The dangers of such inaction, he suggested, were to be seen in the status of the Macedo-Romanians, or Aromanians, *a numerous population of the Romanian race*, living in former Ottoman territory, which had now been divided among the Balkan allies. Brătianu's immediate interest in their largely overlooked cause seems to have been as leverage for Romania to use to gain concessions from the victorious Balkan allies. He would have preferred that they remain in the Ottoman Empire, a *tolerant state* which had been supportive of the Romanian government's measures to improve their education and general well-being. That Ottoman cover, he thought, had been important because the Macedo-Romanians, or at least the educated among them, had reached a *preliminary stage* in the *rebirth* of their national sentiment, a delicate condition he was certain would require *much nourishment* in the future. But if, as now seemed likely, they were to be divided among a number of national states, firm measures would have to be taken to assure their cultural and religious identity, a duty, he implied, that Romania was only too ready to assume.[6]

Matters in the Balkans now came to a head. On the night of 29/30 June 1913, Bulgaria attacked its former allies and three days later Carol ordered mobilisation, a decision that was greeted with popular enthusiasm and street demonstrations – interestingly enough against Austria-Hungary, not Bulgaria. A part of the Romanian army crossed the Danube into Bulgaria at Turnu-Măgurele and other points, and another part advanced southward from Dobrudja. Neither met serious resistance, as the main Bulgarian army was engaged on other fronts. On 22 July King Carol and his government agreed to an armistice.

Brătianu took part in the short-lived Bulgarian campaign as a major in an artillery regiment. Although he saw no front-line duty, he was a keen observer of men at war. He was moved by the patriotism and devotion of the peasant soldiers, but also noted their keen observations of the Bulgarian countryside and the contrasts they drew between its relative prosperity and their own low standard of living.[7] This confirmed his belief that urgent action to meet peasant expectations was necessary. He also had a vague presentiment that a European-wide conflict was inevitable, though he did not think it was imminent. In any case, he was persuaded that time should not be lost in preparing the country both morally and materially for fateful events to come.

The outcome of the Balkan Crisis and the Second Balkan War, in particular, proved decisive in the evolution of Romania's relations with the Triple Alliance. It emerged with enhanced prestige and self-confidence, and both Liberals and Conservatives were ready to pursue a foreign policy independent of the will of the Central Powers. The Romanian government was the host in Bucharest for peace negotiations, which were quickly concluded because of Bulgaria's defeat on all fronts. In accordance with the terms of the Treaty of Bucharest of 10 August 1913, Bulgaria ceded southern Dobrudja, the so-called Quadrilateral, to Romania, accepting the line between Turtucaia and Balchik as the new border.

Romania's success added new strains to its relations with Austria-Hungary. Berchtold was upset by the Treaty and pressed for a revision of its terms. His main objective seems still to have been to win Bulgaria to the side of the Triple Alliance and thereby counterbalance what he feared would be an alliance of Balkan states directed against Austria-Hungary. He was certain that Romania, now satisfied in the south, would focus its attention on Transylvania, and that Serbia would also turn north in pursuit of its irredentist ambitions among the large Serbian population of southern Hungary. In the end, he dropped his objections to the Treaty, but he had done further damage to relations with Romania.

The alienation of Romania from Austria-Hungary now seemed irreversible to many in both Vienna and Bucharest. Graf Ottokar Czernin, the newly-appointed Austro-Hungarian Minister to Romania, shared this view; but he still hoped to keep Romania from joining the Triple Entente, the alliance formed by agreements between France and Russia in 1893, Britain and France in 1904 and Britain and Russia in 1907. For this to happen, he urged that the Hungarian government be persuaded to change drastically the intransigent, nationalist policy it had been pursuing toward the Romanians in Transylvania. His assessment of the mood among politicians in Bucharest was remarkably accurate. Support for the Triple Alliance had so wasted away by the end of 1913 that only King Carol and a few Conservatives, though much aggrieved by the behaviour of Austria-Hungary, still put their hopes in a Germanophile policy as the best course to follow.

The coming to power of Ionel Brătianu and the Liberals in January 1914 signalled a reorientation of Romania's foreign policy. The achievement of national goals was his primary focus. But, true to his political instincts and guided by his experience of the small power-Great Power imbalance in international relations, he embraced caution.

A growing irritant in Austro-Hungarian-Romanian relations was the status of the Romanians of Transylvania. It had become a state-to-state issue in the 1890s as relations between the Romanian National Party, which had represented the Romanian cause in Transylvania since its founding in 1881, and the Hungarian government steadily worsened. A leading National Party spokesman and a deputy in the Hungarian

Parliament, Iuliu Maniu (1873–1953), put the Romanian case succinctly in a speech in Parliament in 1906. He proclaimed the right of every nationality to develop in accordance with its own inherent nature, and to ensure fulfilment of that right he urged a thorough restructuring of Austria-Hungary to provide an appropriate environment of freedom and justice. In effect, he was advocating national autonomy for all the peoples of Austria-Hungary and proposed federalisation as the most appropriate means of satisfying their aspirations.[8]

The Romanian government and Romanian politicians from both major parties became deeply involved in the matter from the 1890s on. Undoubtedly, many Liberals and Conservatives were guided in part by national feeling and the desire to defend the interests of Romanian 'brothers', but they displayed a less altruistic side, too: they were eager to use the confrontation between the Hungarian government and the Romanians of Transylvania to further Romania's foreign-policy objectives and to gain political advantage over one another at home by playing upon the nationalist passions of the electorate. An attempt at conciliation with the Romanian National Party in Transylvania promoted by István Tisza (1861–1918), perhaps the most influential political figure in Hungary of the day, between 1910 and 1913 ultimately failed because neither he nor the leaders of the Romanian National Party could agree on the level of autonomy to be granted the Romanians.

Ionel Brătianu's approach to the Transylvania issue was one of prudence. On the one hand, he thought it essential that Romania preserve its links with the Central Powers in the absence of any other reliable patron. Yet, on the other, he could not ignore the mounting pressure of Romanian public opinion and of politicians within his own party for action to defend the rights of 'brothers' across the mountains. Accordingly, in meetings with Transylvanian Romanian leaders he urged them to follow a policy of moderation until Romania's international alignments could be changed. He supported the talks between the National Party and Tisza as a welcome means of reducing tensions between Romania and Austria-Hungary,[9] but he also seems to have had in mind establishing a link between Romania's foreign policy objectives during the Balkan Crisis and the grievances of the Transylvanian Romanians.

Officials in Vienna and Bucharest had observed the negotiations between Tisza and the Romanian National Party with growing anxiety. On the Austrian side, those in charge of foreign policy and others who were concerned about the future of the Empire strove desperately to maintain Romania's links to the Triple Alliance. First among them was the heir to the throne, Archduke Franz Ferdinand. His attitude on the nationality question in Hungary, which Romanian leaders in Transylvania interpreted as favouring some sort of federalisation of the Monarchy, encouraged them to hope for forceful intervention from Vienna on their behalf.

In Bucharest, one of Franz Ferdinand's associates, Czernin, who may well have owed his appointment as Minister to Romania to the Archduke's intervention, had been astonished by the depth of ill-feeling toward the Dual Monarchy which he encountered on all sides. Czernin (and other Austrian officials) attributed this hostile atmosphere in large measure to the nationality policy of the Hungarian government, and he advised his superiors in Vienna in December 1913 that unless a solution were found quickly the treaty with Romania 'would not be worth the paper it was written on'.[10] He urged Franz Ferdinand to use his influence in both Vienna and Bucharest to foster a Hungarian-Romanian rapprochement and thereby preserve Romania as an ally of the Central Powers.

The expectations in Vienna and Bucharest of a break-through in the Tisza-National Party negotiations proved illusory. Brătianu seems to have been genuinely upset by the lack of progress. It reinforced his sense of foreboding about the situation in Central Europe and the Balkans and persuaded him that the failure of the Tisza-National Party talks made a rapprochement with Austria-Hungary more difficult, at least in the short run. On 15 July 1913 he warned Graf von Waldburg, First Secretary of the German Legation in Bucharest, that Austro-Hungarian leaders were making a serious mistake if they continued to tolerate the ill-treatment of the Romanians of Transylvania. He thought relations with Romania had been so adversely affected that no Romanian government, of whatever party, could contemplate standing side-by-side with Austria-Hungary in the event of war.[11]

A noticeable shift in Romania's foreign policy occurred after Brătianu became Prime Minister in January 1914. Yet, he contemplated no abrupt changes in Romania's international commitments, for he was certain of the Central Powers' military superiority over the Entente and, despite occasional wishful thinking, he saw no likelihood of Austria-Hungary's collapse in the foreseeable future. Unlike his Conservative predecessors, Petre Carp and Titu Maiorescu, however, he was more receptive to French and Russian overtures, and King Carol did not object to an improvement of relations with the Entente, especially Russia. Relations with France had warmed perceptibly during the latter phases of the Balkan crisis, as French diplomats supported Romania's armed intervention in the Second Balkan War, approved of the provisions of the Treaty of Bucharest and opposed Austria-Hungary's efforts to call an international conference to revise it. On the Russian side, Foreign Minister Sergey Sazonov eagerly took advantage of the strain in relations between Romania and Austria-Hungary to pursue a rapprochement with Romania, which had gone nowhere with the pro-German Conservatives in power in Bucharest. He undertook to coordinate his own initiatives with those of his French colleagues in a joint effort to woo Romania away from the Triple Alliance.

A significant breakthrough was the visit of Tsar Nicholas II to Constanța on 14 June 1914 in response to an invitation from King Carol and with Brătianu's full blessing. The two sides agreed to maintain inviolate the provisions of the Treaty of Bucharest, thereby reassuring the Romanians of Russian benevolence in their relations with Bulgaria; and they decided to cooperate in promoting their respective commercial interests in the Black Sea. But Brătianu rejected all proposals that would commit Romania unequivocally to the Triple Entente. He was more than willing to proceed with an improvement in relations with Russia, but he was wary of adding new strains to relations with Austria-Hungary and continued to express the utmost respect for Germany's military and economic might.

His strategy now was to avoid jeopardising gains already achieved; he would expand contacts with France and Russia without causing a rupture with Austria-Hungary and Germany. But the assassination of Archduke Franz Ferdinand on 28 June upset all Brătianu's calculations. He had placed great hopes in the Archduke for a change in the status of the Transylvanian Romanians and a consequent softening of hostility toward Austria-Hungary. He now looked to the future with mixed feelings of trepidation and expectation.

4

Neutrality, 1914–1916

In the month that followed the assassination of Archduke Franz Ferdinand, Brătianu, King Carol and leading Liberal and Conservative politicians became more and more anxious as they watched the Great Powers move inexorably toward war – with good reason. First of all, their country, situated between Austria-Hungary and Russia, might become involved in a major conflict and even be turned into a battlefield. Then, they knew that the Romanian army was unprepared to fight a modern war. They were also troubled by rifts within the political establishment itself, as the King and a small but influential group of Germanophiles favoured the Central Powers, while a majority of politicians and public opinion supported the Entente. Both Brătianu and the King disapproved of Austria-Hungary's aggressive behaviour toward Serbia and both urged the two sides to settle their differences through negotiation. But they became convinced war was inevitable when on 24 July they learned the contents of Austria-Hungary's ultimatum to Serbia. They were certain Serbia would have no choice but to reject its harsh terms and that Russia would surely come to its defence, if it were attacked.

Europe 1914

Petrograd (St Petersburg)

Riga

Moscow

Vilna

nigsberg

RUSSIAN EMPIRE

arsaw

Brest-Litovsk

Kiev

est

Odessa

ROMANIA

Bucharest

Black Sea

BULGARIA

Sofia

BIA

Constantinople

GREECE

OTTOMAN EMPIRE

Athens

Both Brătianu and the King were anxious to prevent the outbreak of a general European war. But if war came, Carol would prefer to fulfil Romania's obligations to the Triple Alliance. Nonetheless, as he informed Czernin on 24 July, too many 'untoward events' had occurred in recent years and the internal situation in Romania was too volatile for him to contemplate seriously entering the War on the side of the Central Powers. The best he could offer was strict neutrality. Such a policy coincided with Brătianu's immediate aims. Nor, it seems, did Austro-Hungarian leaders hope for anything more. Conrad von Hötzendorf, Chief of the General Staff of the Austro-Hungarian army, spoke for many of his colleagues when he admitted he had no illusions about where the majority of Romanian politicians' sympathies lay; he expected no help from them because their supreme goal was to unite all Romanians in a national state by annexing Transylvania and Bukovina.

There can be little doubt that the formation of Greater Romania was Brătianu's paramount long-term ambition. But as the crisis deepened he was forced again to turn to relations with Bulgaria and decide how best to maintain the coveted Balkan equilibrium. The Treaty of Bucharest had by no means ended the rivalry with Bulgaria, but had, instead, left a deeply aggrieved neighbour on Romania's Danube frontier. At a meeting on 27 July with Czernin, who continued to try to extract a clear statement of the Liberal government's intentions, Brătianu let it be known he would follow a policy of 'watching and waiting'. Yet, he was unequivocal on one matter: if Bulgaria entered the War and if there were significant changes in the balance of power in South-eastern Europe, Romania would be obliged to re-examine its commitment to neutrality. If, as he expected, Austria-Hungary prevailed over

Serbia and Bulgaria shared in the spoils, then he left no doubt that Romania would seek territorial compensation.[1]

The policy advocated by Brătianu and the majority of politicians – neutrality – prevailed at a meeting of the Crown Council at Sinaia, the royal summer residence in the Carpathian Mountains north of Bucharest, on 3 August 1914. Two issues were on the table at this solemn gathering of the Cabinet members, former Prime Ministers and important political leaders presided over by the King. The first was whether to respect treaty commitments to the Central Powers and, consequently, whether to enter the War immediately on their side. Only the King and Petre Carp spoke in favour of such a course. Brătianu spoke for the majority when he called attention to the overwhelming public support for the Entente and for the Romanians of Transylvania. He also gave cover to those who might have had qualms about violating the terms of the alliance with the Central Powers by pointing out that the Austro-Hungarian government itself had relieved the Romanian government of any obligations it had; it had failed to notify the Romanian government beforehand of its intention to present an ultimatum to Serbia, negligence that clearly breached the Treaty. He also thought the ultimatum had been designed to provoke a conflict, as no sovereign state could have accepted its punitive terms. The other choice before the Council – a declaration of neutrality – had the unequivocal support of the majority. King Carol, acknowledging himself to be a constitutional monarch, reluctantly acquiesced.[2]

The decision of the Crown Council came as no surprise to the Central Powers. Both Austria-Hungary and Germany in the next two years applied constant pressure on Brătianu to join them. The death of King Carol on 10 October was viewed in Vienna and Berlin as disastrous. They expected no sympathy from Brătianu, whose preference for the Entente they well knew and even exaggerated; and they were uncertain about where the new King, Carol's nephew Ferdinand, stood on the vital issues that concerned them. Czernin, in Bucharest, was particularly disheartened. He was convinced that if the War went against the Central Powers, Romania would attack Austria-Hungary.[3] Yet Brătianu remained the pragmatist. He was not prepared to abandon neutrality until the fortunes of war were clearer. He sought to placate both sides and he kept his own counsel.

Carol's death left Brătianu in charge of foreign policy and the person most responsible for the fate of the country. King Ferdinand was pro-German, but he lacked his uncle's strong will to promote a policy at odds with the ambitions of the majority of politicians and the mood of the public. Moreover, he showed great confidence in Brătianu's abilities. His wife, Marie, was more forceful. She made no secret in private of her Entente sympathies and promoted its cause in many subtle ways.[4] Brătianu was careful to keep Ferdinand informed of events and of his own thinking and consulted him frequently. But he was determined to direct foreign policy with a minimum of interference. He chose as his Foreign Minister between 1914 and 1916, Emanoil Porumbacu, who was the consummate follower without goals of his own and thus could serve as a convenient figurehead.

During the autumn of 1914 Brătianu took several important diplomatic initiatives. Italy's reaction to the July crisis, the outbreak of war and decision to remain neutral, despite membership in the Triple Alliance, had reinforced his own advocacy of neutrality. He thus lost no time in concluding a formal accord with Italy. The two governments agreed on 23 September to inform the other beforehand of any shifts in

policy or of any plans to renounce neutrality. Their understanding reflected a common interest in acquiring Austro-
Hungarian territory inhabited by their co-nationals. For
Romania, in particular, it represented a further step away
from engagement with the Central Powers.

Brătianu also negotiated with Russia in Bucharest and
Petrograd in July, and the territorial claims Romania then
advanced are further evidence of Brătianu's intention to
align with the Entente. But he would not commit himself to
a course of action until the time seemed right. Sazonov, the
Russian Foreign Minister, took the initiative. On 5 August
he gave the Romanian Minister in Petrograd Constantin
Diamandy the preliminary text of a convention between the
two countries covering military cooperation and territorial
issues. Romania would commit all its forces against Austria-
Hungary as soon as the treaty came into effect and not make
a separate peace with Austria-Hungary without Russia's
consent. In return, Russia agreed not to make peace until all
of Austria-Hungary's territories inhabited by Romanians had
been united with Romania. Sazonov promised that Russia
would guarantee Romania's territorial integrity if Bulgaria
attacked. Brătianu found the proposals attractive, but he had
no intention of entering the conflict before its outcome had
become predictable. He was well aware that the deep enmity
felt by Romanians toward Russia and the ingrained suspi-
cion of its intentions in South-eastern Europe could not be
brushed aside lightly. Neither could he shake his own distrust
of Russia, which his knowledge of Russo-Romanian relations
in the 19th century had nourished. He was thus eager to have
France and Britain as parties to any accord with Russia, but
neither seemed to think much of Sazonov's undertaking;
Romania struck them as still too committed politically and

economically to the Central Powers, and they worried that a Russian-Romanian alliance might upset the balance of forces in the Balkans and lead Bulgaria and Turkey to attack Greece and Serbia.

Sazonov persisted with a new Russian offer on 26 September, requiring much less of Romania. In exchange for Romania's benevolent neutrality, Russia would accept the union with Romania of Austro-Hungarian territory inhabited by Romanians. It further stipulated that the new boundaries would be drawn on the basis of ethnicity, a subtle reminder of Russia's claims to northern Bukovina, a part of Moldavia seized by Austria in 1774 whose majority was Slavic.[5] Sazonov thus no longer sought Romania's military intervention, perhaps because the Russian High Command was reluctant to open a new front in the south and had serious doubts about the capabilities of the Romanian army. Still others in the Russian government worried that Sazonov's embrace of ethnic principles in Austria-Hungary and his promotion of a Romanian national state might lead to questions about the future of Bessarabia, the region of Moldavia between the Prut and Dniester Rivers that Russia had annexed in 1812 and had subjected to unrelenting Russification, and which had thus become a persistent sore point in Russo-Romanian relations. When Sazonov put the matter of Bessarabia to Diamandy, he equivocated, limiting himself to the hope that Sazonov's policies would create a new atmosphere of 'mutual confidence'. Despite misgivings and a lack of warmth, both sides wanted some kind of an agreement, and on 1 October letters were exchanged between Sazonov and Diamandy along the lines of the Russian proposal of 26 September. But now Sazonov added two stipulations. First, Russia's opposition to any violation of Romania's territory would be by diplomatic rather than military action; and second, Romania's benevolent neutrality would mean that it would prevent the transit of military supplies for the Central Powers across its territory, but would facilitate shipments from Russia to Serbia.[6] Brătianu, who had directed Romania's negotiations with the authority of King Carol, approved the first proposition so long as cooperation between the two governments was based on a diplomatic and not a military understanding, but he insisted that as soon as Romania entered the War against Austria-Hungary Russia would have to support Romania by substantial military means. On the movement of war materiel across his country Brătianu avoided a direct answer, observing merely that interference with shipments to and from the Central Powers might make it difficult for Romania to arm herself.

Between autumn 1914 and summer 1916, when Romania finally entered the War on the side of the Entente, Brătianu was under constant pressure to act, both from the inside, especially from militants across the political spectrum who demanded immediate intervention against Austria-Hungary, and from outside, from both the Central Powers and the Entente. His ability to resist and his perseverance in following the path he had chosen were remarkable. He had to take into account the shifting fortunes on the battlefronts in the East and in the West, and had to make certain that the rewards would justify the fateful decision for war. Not the least of his worries was the state of the country's economy and the readiness of the Romanian army for an extended campaign.

During the years of neutrality the War largely shaped the course of domestic politics. Significant divisions arose within both of the main parties about what policies to pursue. The strain within the Conservative Party became critical, as the tensions evident since the turn of the century were aggravated by the outbreak of the War and the need to take a firm stand on involvement or neutrality. Rivalries over party leadership added to the disarray. The group led by Titu Maiorescu and Alexandru Marghiloman favoured neutrality and caused Brătianu little trouble; but a smaller, noisier group centred around Nicolae Filipescu, an uncompromising critic of the Liberals, and Take Ionescu and his Democratic Conservatives, demanded immediate military intervention against Austria-Hungary. Their constant clamour was worrisome to Brătianu because they were drawing a broader public, *the street*, as he called it, into the controversy, an element that was unpredictable and difficult to control. All these diverse elements were united by a single urge to 'liberate' the Romanians of Transylvania and bring about 'national unity' as quickly as possible. Relations between Brătianu, Maiorescu and Marghiloman became increasingly strained as the Conservatives tried to force him from office on the grounds he was endangering the country's security by refusing to negotiate with the Central Powers. They had no success as they could overcome neither Brătianu's stubbornness nor King Ferdinand's weakness. Animosities within the Conservative Party reached the breaking-point at the opening of Parliament in November 1915.[7] By contrast, the Liberal Party, under Brătianu's stern direction, was far more united than the Conservatives and the majority, favourable to the Entente, supported his policy of neutrality.

Neutrality, benevolent or otherwise, did not spare the Romanian economy; and managing it became, alongside intensified political strife, Brătianu's chief domestic concern. Agriculture was severely affected by mobilisation, which deprived smallholders of manpower. They also bore the brunt of government requisitioning of animals and foodstuffs and the disruption of traditional markets. Industry, now called upon to produce more and more weapons and equipment for the army, could not supply all that was needed because of the lack of capacity and the shortage of skilled labour. Government funds for industrial development became tighter and tighter, foreign investment nearly ceased and domestic credit was inadequate to cover even normal needs, let alone pay for increased quantities of armaments.

The country's foreign trade was also adversely affected. Before the outbreak of the War almost 80 per cent passed through the Black Sea and the Straits. Turkey's closing of the Straits in 1914 severely limited Romania's flourishing commerce with France, Britain and the Low Countries and in effect made it more dependent on the Central Powers. In 1914 Germany and Austria-Hungary were already major trading partners with Romania. During the two years of neutrality Germany's share of its trade went from 23 to nearly 30 per cent and Austria-Hungary's from 18 to 48 per cent. For its part, Romania exported large quantities of grain and oil to the Central Powers, who, because of the demands of war, were anxious to maintain and even expand access to these valuable resources. In return, Romania wanted military equipment of all kinds, but, suspicious of the Brătianu government's long-term intentions, the Central Powers offered only a small part of what was requested.

Brătianu's way of dealing with economic and financial adversity was to expand the government's role. His immediate aim was to assure sufficient quantities of food for the general population and the army and adequate raw materials to maintain industrial production. Decrees in 1914 and 1915 temporarily limited exports of essential items; and in 1916, as food stocks dwindled, these restrictions were made permanent. The government established commissions to prevent speculation in goods in short supply by fixing prices on many foodstuffs, to supervise trade in grains and to provide villages with sufficient quantities of maize, the basic food in the countryside. As for the credit crisis, the government turned secretly to Britain and Italy for loans to cover both its regular needs and the new expenditures caused by increased armament production. Britain responded with loans amounting to £12 million for the purchase of military equipment from British companies. To expand the domestic production of guns and ammunition the government in 1915 created the Technical Industrial Commission to oversee war production. All these initiatives in some measure eased the hardships felt in every sector of the economy and at every level of society, especially among the peasant majority. But the pressures of war, even for a neutral country, became more acute as time passed. Brătianu had no control over the course of events; in frustration, he could only react.

Perhaps the heaviest burden Brătianu had to bear as the War continued was diplomatic. Both sides used inducements and threats to force him to abandon neutrality in their favour. Relations with the Central Powers were continually tense, despite the considerable quantities of grain and oil that Romania supplied to them and the efforts by politicians in Vienna and Berlin to persuade István Tisza, now Prime Minister of Hungary, to make meaningful concessions to the Romanians of Transylvania. Tisza adamantly rejected any compromise with the Romanians, and although Czernin's reports from Bucharest were uniformly discouraging in 1914 and 1915, hope lingered that somehow Romanian political leaders, other than Brătianu, could be persuaded to join the war on the side of the Central Powers.[8]

Brătianu's relations with the Entente were no less stressful than those with the Central Powers, even though the course that Romania must inevitably follow, an alliance with France and Britain, seemed clear to him. He continued his negotiations with the Entente through Russia, but their course was far from satisfactory. The Russian High Command had little interest in 1915 in Romania's entrance into the War, because of continued uncertainty about the effectiveness of the Romanian army. Russian officials in general thought Brătianu wanted too high a price for Romania's cooperation with the Entente; and, in any case, they were unwilling to strengthen Romania's position in a zone they had marked out for Russian predominance. On the Romanian side, Brătianu was still reluctant to join the Entente solely through a bilateral treaty with Russia; he wanted France and Britain to be fully committed to support Romania's war effort and ready to guarantee the satisfaction of Romania's territorial claims on Austria-Hungary. He seems also to have opposed Russia's pretensions to Constantinople and the Straits in order to prevent an overwhelming Russian presence in the Balkans, which he continued to think was an area of special interest to Romania. In 1915, consequently, there was little movement toward a formal agreement. When Brătianu had Diamandy present his conditions for entry into the War to Sazonov at the beginning of May 1915, Sazonov thought them excessive and the Russian High Command urged him not to abandon Russia's strategic interests in South-eastern Europe and the Straits in return for a military alliance of doubtful value.

Throughout his negotiations with the Entente, Brătianu also maintained regular contact with Italian leaders. Following a line of thought that had persuaded him to conclude the agreement of September 1914, he was certain that a common front in dealing with France and Britain would improve Romania's own prospects of achieving its territorial ambitions. On 6 February 1915 he and Baron Carlo Fasciotti, the Italian Minister to Romania between 1911 and 1919, signed a memorandum in which the two countries pledged to support one another in case their territorial integrity was affected by international 'complications'. Yet, despite these contacts, Romania was left out of the final negotiations which led to the signing of the Treaty of London of 26 April 1915, by which Italy agreed to join the War on the side of the Entente. When Italy did declare war on Austria-Hungary on 23 May 1915 and on Germany 15 months later on 28 August 1916, pressure on Brătianu from the interventionists in Bucharest intensified. But he remained firm; though he knew he could not afford to be overtaken by events, the right moment had not yet arrived.

By the spring of 1916 France and Russia were determined to use all possible means to secure Romania's commitment to the Entente war effort in time to coincide with the general offensive being planned on both the Western and Russian fronts. On 16 June Camille Blondel, the French Minister in Bucharest, put the matter bluntly to Brătianu that the time for decision had come. Brătianu himself had already reached the same conclusion. He grasped the critical nature of the moment and realised a policy of neutrality could no longer be sustained, if he hoped to bring into being a united Romanian national state.[9] Yet, he held back. Romania's geographical isolation from the Western Allies was a continual source of anxiety. To enter the War without guarantees of regular supplies of munitions and equipment was for him (and many other Romanians) to expose the country to incalculable danger. Events of the past year had done little to calm his fears. The Allies' abandonment of the Gallipoli campaign in January 1916 meant the Straits, the most accessible route for supplies to reach Romania from the West, would remain closed to Allied shipping. The failure of Allied commanders at Salonica to launch a sustained attack against Bulgaria, which had entered the War on the side of the Central Powers in October 1915, and then proceed northward to the Danube suggested to Brătianu that the Romanian army would have to fight simultaneously on two fronts – the Austro-Hungarian and Bulgarian – a situation he thought would be disastrous.

As Brătianu's negotiations with Russia and France continued he insisted they fulfil a series of conditions. He wanted guarantees that Russia and Italy would provide 300 tons of war materiel a day for the duration of the War; that a coordinated Allied offensive on all fronts would begin at the same time as the Romanian attack on Austria-Hungary, particularly a Russian offensive in Galicia and Bukovina to buttress Romania's northern flank; and that sufficient Russian forces be dispatched to Dobrudja to protect Romania's southern flank against Bulgaria, or, if this proved impossible, that an Allied offensive against Bulgaria from Salonica be undertaken. He also insisted the Allies and Romania sign a political treaty specifying the territory Romania would receive from Austria-Hungary at the end of the War, notably Transylvania, Bukovina, and the Banat, as he had indicated in his negotiations with Russia in 1915. He presented his conditions to Blondel on 4 July and promised that if they were accepted, Romania would begin military operations in early August.[10]

Negotiations went on for another six weeks, and throughout this tense period Brătianu was beset by doubts as to whether he had chosen the right course. On the one hand, he was deterred from taking bold action by Romania's isolation from the Western Allies and the limited capabilities of its army. On the other hand, he had to take into account the shifting fortunes of the belligerents on the battlefield. In the late spring of 1916 it seemed to him that his plans for Greater Romania might be undone not by war but by peace. Rumours were circulating about peace-feelers from the Central Powers in the wake of the successful Russian offensive in Galicia in June and July, which had revealed the weakness of the Austro-Hungarian army. He was afraid that if the belligerents in fact decided to make peace before Romania entered the War, then it would not have 'earned' the right to have a say in the redrawing of territorial boundaries and thus would have lost the opportunity to consolidate the Romanian national state.

Another thought was uppermost in his mind, too. If the War continued and France and Britain were the victors, then he was certain he would need their support at the peace conference in order to acquire Austro-Hungarian territories inhabited by Romanians. That support, he knew, could only be won on the battlefield. National ambitions, in the end, outweighed all other considerations in his decision for war.

It was precisely at this moment in June 1916 that Russia and France exerted all their powers of persuasion on Brătianu. In effect, they gave him an ultimatum: unless he entered the War immediately, he could not hope to achieve his territorial ambitions. Britain backed the Franco-Russian initiative, but played only a minor role in the proceedings, as generally since the end of 1915 it had left the initiative in the Balkans to others.[11] The delays in reaching a final accord with Brătianu seem to have been due mainly to the long-standing reluctance of Russian politicians to satisfy all his territorial and military demands which they thought 'exaggerated', and by the objections of Russian military commanders to extending the war front to the south. At last, the French offered a formula which softened Russian resistance and opened the way to an agreement, but for obvious reasons they kept it from Brătianu. They proposed that Russia and the other Allies accept for the time being all Brătianu's conditions, even the one they found most objectionable (that Romania be accorded equal status with the principal Allies at the peace conference); then, at the end of the War, if they found they could not satisfy all his demands, they would simply force him to make do with less than they had promised.[12] The way was thus cleared for a formal treaty. On 17 August 1916 Brătianu and the representatives of France, Britain, Russia and Italy in Bucharest signed military and political conventions specifying the conditions for Romania's entrance into the War. Most important for Brătianu were those articles setting a date for Romania's launching an attack on Austria-Hungary of not later than 28 August and recognising the right of the Romanians of Transylvania, Bukovina and the Banat to choose union with the Romanian Kingdom at the end of the War. For good reason nothing was said of Bessarabia.

5
War, 1916–1918

Brătianu had delayed entrance into the War as long as he could, but pressure from the Allies, especially their warnings of 'now or never' with the clear implication that inaction would thwart his ambitions for national unity, had at last become irresistible and he had yielded. But he was painfully aware that he had not been able to choose the right moment. In the days following the signing of the accords with the Entente he was wracked by doubts. His sombre mood was justified by the events of the next few months. The projected Allied advance north from Salonica was delayed, and, instead, he could expect a determined Bulgarian attack from the south. Nor had the projected offensive on the Russian front materialised, and deliveries of military supplies from the West through Russia were inadequate and intermittent. Another source of anxiety was the need to maintain complete secrecy about the military action Romania was about to take. Czernin was certain that something dramatic was afoot and used every lever at his disposal to discover what Brătianu was up to. He met with Brătianu himself and other politicians at regular intervals and made a special effort to influence King Ferdinand, who he thought was still committed to the Central Powers.

As he often did in times of stress, Brătianu left the political cauldron that was Bucharest for the shelter of his vineyards and library at Florica. After a few days of rest and pondering the grave moment at which the country found itself, he returned to the capital a week before the fateful declaration of war.

The final decision for war on the side of the Entente came at a meeting of the Crown Council at Cotroceni Palace in Bucharest on 27 August 1916. It would be more accurate to say that the Council had been summoned to ratify a decision already taken, since Brătianu and the King, who now fully supported him, presented their colleagues with a fait accompli. Yet, the debate was no less spirited as the opponents of intervention on the side of the Entente argued passionately for continued neutrality. Petre Carp, the most obstinate, insisted that to join Russia on the battlefield was to strike a blow at the very existence of the country. Overcome with emotion, as he sensed that he stood alone, he declared that he had three sons who he would now give to the King to die; he himself would pray to God that the Romanian army be defeated 'because only in this way can Romania be saved'.[1] The members of the Council were stunned, as Carp refused to reconsider his words, even at the urging of the King. Finally, Brătianu could no longer contain himself and told Carp to take his sons out of the army because he, Carp, no longer had anything to share with his country and its people.[2]

As the debate continued, Titu Maiorescu expressed puzzlement at the abandonment of the policy of watchful waiting and urged that Romania disengage from its hasty alliance with the Entente. Alexandru Marghiloman also thought Brătianu's initiative rash and was pessimistic about the chances of success. Brătianu responded forcefully. He expressed full confidence in the victory of the Entente and the realisation of their country's national destiny. He drew his colleagues' attention to the terms of the agreement signed the week before by Romania and its four allies: *They recognised our rights to take [Austro-Hungarian] territory up to the Tisza River, the Banat, Crişana, the lower, non-Slavic parts of Maramureş, and Bukovina as far as the Prut River, and they recognised our equal rights at the peace conference.*[3]

'...they recognised our equal rights at the peace conference'

BRĂTIANU, 27 AUGUST 1916

He then spoke in more sombre tones. He admitted they might fail, but argued that the country at this fateful moment in its history had no choice but to follow the course he had recommended to the King. They must take the long view of history and not be diverted from their *preordained path* by thoughts of failure. If they suffered defeat, it would be only temporary. He pointed to the movements of the Germans and Italians for unification in the 19th century as models to be emulated; along the way they, too, had experienced setbacks, but, in the end, they had reached their goals. There were times in the lives of nations, he warned, when the failure to seize the moment and act, however high the stakes and risky the outcome, was an abdication of responsibility by its leaders, a *moral betrayal*. He took full responsibility for the course he had laid before them.[4] The King stood solidly behind him. When the final vote came, all except Petre Carp approved Brătianu's decision to enter the War on the side of the Allies.

On the walk home from the meeting accompanied by his close adviser Ion G Duca, and speaking more to himself than to his companion, Brătianu repeated several times that *severe trials* (*grele încercări*) lay ahead, but that they could not have acted otherwise. Then, to Duca directly he said matter-of-factly: *Let's get to work. At four, the Council of Ministers at your house.*[5]

In the evening of 27 August the Romanian Minister in Vienna presented his country's declaration of war at the Austro-Hungarian Foreign Ministry. A short time later, in the night of the 27th, Romanian troops began to cross the border into Transylvania. Austria-Hungary, followed by Germany, on the 28th declared war on Romania, as did their allies, Turkey on the 30th and Bulgaria on 1 September.

The Allied plan for the Romanian army was to coordinate its operations with general Allied offensives on the Western and Russian Fronts. Its tasks were to drive enemy forces from Transylvania and then proceed through Hungary to the Tisza River and through the Banat to the Danube thereby depriving Austro-Hungarian forces of their chief sources of food and other agricultural supplies. Nearly three-quarters of the army's total force of 575,000, or roughly 420,000 men, were committed to the campaign. In the south the army's goals were less ambitious: to hold the frontier against an attack by Bulgarian forces

Ion G Duca (1879–1933), a lawyer with a law degree from Paris and a skilled politician, was one of the chief theorists of Neo-Liberalism and one of Ionel Brătianu's closest collaborators and advisers. He was a Minister in numerous Liberal governments; and as Minister of Foreign Affairs (1922–6), he played a leading role in formulating Romanian foreign policy as a supporter of collective security, an advocate of settling international disputes peacefully and a promoter of the Little Entente. He became President of the Liberal Party in 1930 succeeding Vintilă Brătianu and Prime Minister in 1933. A staunch opponent of the extreme right, he dissolved the Iron Guard in 1933, and in revenge the Guard assassinated him shortly afterwards.

and a German expeditionary army, all under the command of German Field Marshal August von Mackensen, until Russian troops could be landed in Dobrudja. The combined Romanian-Russian army would then take the offensive and establish a fortified defence line running from Ruschuk on the Danube to Varna on the Black Sea. The Romanians committed roughly 140,000 men to this operation.

Brătianu had good reason to worry that his army was not up to the tasks assigned to it. It was indeed a large force, but it lacked sufficient equipment and munitions. Despite Brătianu's efforts to expand war production in the preceding two years, Romanian industry had proved incapable of meeting the army's needs. He had had to resort to purchases from abroad, and Austria-Hungary and Germany had been his main suppliers. As he had moved closer to the Entente after the outbreak of war in 1914, and as he sought to reduce the army's dependence on the Central Powers and as they themselves limited the quantity of goods with which they would provide Romania, he turned to the Allies. He signed the first of a number of contracts with France in March 1915, but the transport of supplies from the West was difficult. The route along the Danube from Salonica had been cut when Bulgaria attacked Serbia in October 1915 and the circuitous supply lines through Archangel on the White Sea and Vladivostok on the Pacific were undependable.

The Romanian army thus undertook its first major campaign since the War for Independence in 1877–8 with inadequate equipment and uncertain of its sources of essential provisions. A Romanian division, for example, had only three or four field artillery pieces per battery and a few heavy machine-guns, whereas Austro-Hungarian and German divisions had at least double that number. Inadequacies of transport made the movement of troops to different battle-fronts and their reinforcement cumbersome and slow; the rail-road network, upon which these services mainly depended, had been designed with other purposes in mind. There were also too few well-trained, experienced officers and non-commissioned officers to provide leadership in the field, a deficiency that large-scale, rapid mobilisation had compounded.

Romanian military operations, at first, proceeded according to plan. Romanian troops, meeting only token resistance, occupied Brassó (Braşov) on 30 August and by 2 September had taken possession of the most important Carpathian passes. Within a week the small cities of Fogaras (Făgăraş), Csík-szereda (Miercurea Ciuc) and Székelyudvarhely (Odorhei) had fallen, and the important economic and cultural centre Nagyszeben (Sibiu) was threatened. But abruptly, on 8 September, the high command halted the offensive. Not only had the army's advance been slower than anticipated thus allowing the enemy to reinforce its defensive positions and prepare for a counter-attack, but events in the south had taken an alarming turn. Bulgarian and German forces under Mackensen had gone on the offensive on 31 August and within a week had inflicted a severe defeat on Romanian forces at Turtucaia, just south of the Danube near the Bulgarian border, and had taken Silistria. The Romanian response was to rush troops from the Transylvanian front to strengthen defences, a tactic that was successful in slowing the enemy thrust into Dobrudja and finally stopping it just south of Constanţa on 19 September. General Alexandru Averescu, the new commander in the south, undertook a bold counter-offensive from near Giurgiu across the Danube into northern Bulgaria on 1 October. It was initially successful, but on the 4th he withdrew his forces back across the Danube in order to blunt an Austro-German offensive on the northern front that had steadily gained momentum and threatened to roll Romanian troops back across the Carpathians. These stunning military reverses were a great shock to Brătianu and momentarily shattered his confidence in the outcome of his enterprise. What seems to have been even harder for him to take was the failure of the Allies to honour their commitments.

The Romanian army, under Averescu, was able to maintain a defensive line in the passes along the Carpathians until the end of October, despite heavy enemy pressure. Austro-German forces under German General Erich von Falkenhayn, who had assumed supreme command in Transylvania on 30 September, tried to invade Moldavia through the eastern Carpathian passes in late October, but were repulsed. About the same time at the western end of the Carpathians, stubborn Romanian resistance halted another German attack along the Jiu River.

Brătianu followed the course of events anxiously and took what measures he could to improve chances for success. He had appointed his brother Vintilă, a skilled administrator, as Minister of War on 5 August, a post he himself had held since becoming Prime Minister in 1914. He recognised that the overall coordination of the war effort along with the mobilisation of the home front would leave him little time for the close management of war's administrative details. He was more at home with grand conceptions and broad planning, whereas Vintilă was methodical and attentive to fine points. As the campaigns in Transylvania and the south took their course, the deficiencies of the Romanian army became all too evident. Brătianu was particularly struck by the inability of Romanian officers to cope with the demands of modern war, and he appealed to the French government to send advisers as quickly as possible to provide the officer corps with train-ing and support. In response it dispatched a military mission headed by General Henri Berthelot, which arrived in Bucha-rest at the beginning of October. Berthelot and his large staff, which eventually reached 1,500 men, were to play a key role in the Romanian army's operations for the next year and a half.[6]

As the situation on both the northern and southern fronts worsened and Romanian forces were put on the defensive, Brătianu began to have grave doubts about the sincerity of the promises of support the Allies had used to persuade him to enter the War. On none of the battlefronts had the Allies done enough to relieve the hard-pressed Romanians in Transylvania and Dobrudja. The Russian offensive had been unsuccessful and the Russian military had failed to provide the stipulated contingents for Dobrudja. The per-sonal emissary Brătianu sent to Tsar Nicholas to explain the dire situation at home and to plead for immediate Russian reinforcements had returned empty-handed. The Western Allies had done little more of immediate military value as their promised offensive against Bulgaria from Salonica had been delayed. Brătianu felt not only abandoned but betrayed. He could forgive neither the Allies for making promises which it now appeared they had had little intention of fulfilling nor himself for being taken in and acting upon them when his experience in dealing with the Great Powers had taught him to be wary of their embrace. He found in the present circum-stances confirmation of his often-repeated observations that small states could hope at best to be treated as tools by the Great Powers and must therefore be prepared at every turn to defend their legitimate aspirations without compromise. It was, for him, a fact of international politics which was to guide him throughout the War and at the Peace Conference.

But Brătianu had little time now to dwell on the faults of deceitful allies or to think about questions of grand strategy. On the Transylvanian front Falkenhayn had brought together a powerful force of four infantry and two cavalry divisions along the Jiu River in order to make a decisive breakthrough that would open the way to the Wallachian plain and Bucharest.[7] On 11 November he began the offensive that was to seal Romania's fate and eventually drive it from the War. Opposed by only one Romanian division, his forces took Târgu Jiu on the 17th and Craiova on the 21st. Romanian troops tried to establish a line of defence along the Olt River, but they were overwhelmed by the enemy's superior numbers and firepower. But it was the battle further east along the Argeş and Neajlov Rivers between 30 November and 3 December that was decisive. Romanian forces could not hold the line and began a general retreat eastward. On 25 November the King and on 3 December the government left Bucharest for Iaşi, and on the 6th German troops entered the city. It was not until 10 January 1917 that Romanian units were finally able to establish stable defensive positions extending from the Danube and Siret Rivers in the south to just west of the Siret further north. Thus, a campaign that had begun with such promise with the rapid advance into Transylvania in early September had ended in disaster. Romanian losses in men and equipment had been heavy: 250,000 soldiers killed, wounded or taken prisoner (almost a third of the force mobilised in 1916) and half the army's weapons lost. A recovery seemed out of the question, as over half the country with its most important agricultural lands and its main industrial centres lay in enemy hands.

Ever since the government had left Bucharest Brătianu had been at pains in public to put the best interpretation

possible on the course of events and, in so doing, to preserve some sense of national unity and hope for the future.
On 27 December he spoke before the reassembled Chamber
of Deputies in Iaşi to urge its members not to be discouraged by the turn of events. Finding consolation in history, he
cited Prussia and Italy as countries that had persevered in the
face of defeat. The Germans and the Italians had prevailed,

he insisted, because their causes
had been in accord with the spirit
of the times. That spirit, he was
convinced, was the principle of
nationalism which held the key
to understanding the underlying historical processes that had
been transforming Europe in the
past century. The steady decline
of the Ottoman Empire and the

'... Our victory seems to
me not only a result of the
forces that are now in play
but also as a historical
necessity to anyone who
believes that humankind
has not been created to
go backwards.'

BRĂTIANU, 27 DECEMBER 1916

rise of national states were, he argued, fully in harmony with
the inexorable flow of history. So were the aspirations of the
Romanians to complete the formation of a Romania that
would at last encompass all Romanians: ...*Our victory seems
to me not only a result of the forces that are now in play
but also as a historical necessity to anyone who believes that
humankind has not been created to go backwards.*[8]

Since his arrival in Iaşi, Brătianu had been tireless in his
efforts to restore something like the normal functions of
government, as he had around him his old team of advisers,
including his brother Vintilă and Ion Duca. He thought the
formation of a government of national unity was imperative, and he succeeded in drawing into it Take Ionescu and
his Democratic Conservatives, but the leaders of the various
Conservative factions kept their distance. He set to work at

once to restore the morale of the army and to reassure the populace that their privations would be only temporary. He and his colleagues feared widespread social unrest and even violence unless the physical hardships of war could be alleviated quickly and the mental gloom dissipated. He again made agrarian and electoral reform his immediate domestic concern and revived the legislative initiatives that had been shelved at the outbreak of the War in 1914.

In foreign policy he sought, first of all, to maintain Romania's standing among the Allies. He feared that defeat and military infirmity might lower its status to that of a Serbia and encourage the Allies to think again about the promises they had made in August. An ill-omen was the failure of the Allies to invite Romanian representatives to a conference on war strategy held in Rome in January 1917 at which the campaign at Salonica, of direct interest to Romania, was to be discussed. Brătianu was determined not to be shunted aside; and in the same month he in effect invited himself to a conference in Petrograd where military and supply problems were to be examined by high-level French, British and Russian delegations. He also intended to use the occasion to discuss with his Russian counterparts how best to coordinate military operations in view of the changed circumstances on the Romanian front. He was anxious to persuade them not to withdraw troops from Moldavia, where in reality Russian divisions maintained most of the battle line; and he proposed that the two armies prepare for a major offensive in the spring. But the Russian High Command was reluctant to commit substantial new forces to a sector that was only one among many on the broad front they manned against Germany. Nonetheless, before Brătianu left Petrograd on 10 February he seems to have persuaded Russian political leaders not to make any abrupt changes in the existing line of defence and he counted this as a success.

He was much less satisfied with the treatment his French and British allies accorded him. When he had arrived in Petrograd he had demanded the right to take part in the conference as an equal partner, citing the treaty of alliance he had signed in August. At first, they had rejected his claim outright. Only after considerable manoeuvring did they and the Russians and Italians admit him to their consultations, and then only when Romanian matters came up for discussion. He did, in fact, attend one session at which military questions were debated; and he had private meetings with most of the delegates. But he left Petrograd with a sense of unease, reinforced by his knowledge of European history and his own experience that, despite treaties, the Allies would treat Romania only in ways that furthered their own objectives.[9]

Not long after Brătianu's return home the first Russian Revolution of 1917 in March overturned the Tsarist government. Gone were most of the officials with whom he had so recently struck agreements, and he was now faced with new uncertainties about the maintenance of the battle line in Moldavia and the delivery of supplies. At the end of April, eager to acquaint himself with members of the Provisional Government, he returned to Petrograd for a few days. Conversations with Alexander Kerensky, the leading figure in the new government, were hardly reassuring. Kerensky struck him as weak, too willing to make concessions to the Bolsheviks and unable to resist the general tide of pacifism that was engulfing both the army and the populace. His meeting with the new Minister of War, Alexander Guchkov, also left him deeply troubled. Guchkov warned him that the situation in Russia would continue to deteriorate and predicted that the Provisional Government would be unable to master the situation.[10]

For Brătianu, the disintegration he witnessed in Petrograd and along the way to and from a city in the throes of revolution not only seemed to him the harbinger of disaster on the battlefront in Moldavia, but raised the spectre of widespread, perhaps uncontrollable, protest movements on the home front. He and many of his colleagues were alarmed by the possibility that the 'Bolshevik contagion' would spread across the Prut River and stir revolution among disaffected peasants and soldiers in Moldavia. They were also afraid that Romanian troops would be infected by the growing unrest among Russian troops and would demand radical political and social change. It was in desperation that Brătianu advised the King to issue a proclamation to his peasant soldiers on 5 April, promising them land and the right to vote when the War was over. His initiative had the support of both Liberal and Conservative politicians and did much to restore calm.

Brătianu acknowledged the urgency of the situation by presenting new agrarian and electoral laws to the Chamber of Deputies on 6 May. Like the bills the legislature had considered in the spring of 1914, these would amend the constitution: first, to allow the expropriation of private property by extending the notion of public utility to include land grants to peasants and, second, to extend the franchise to all adult males over 21. The only serious opposition came from the Party of Labour (*Partidul Muncii*), formed on 1 May by a few dissident parliamentary deputies and intellectuals on the left in the Liberal Party who wanted to go further and faster than Brătianu, an impatience which revealed the centrist nature of his Liberalism. In addition to more radical agrarian and electoral reforms, they urged nationalisation of the country's mineral wealth, including oil, a progressive income tax and new labour laws that would authorise collective bargaining between employers and workers and allow strikes. Even though the party was small and had not had time to gather a following among the populace and could not hope to thwart the will of the Liberal majority in Parliament, Brătianu was annoyed. He would not allow the party to publish its program on the grounds that it might lead to social conflict in the prevailing dire circumstances when a sense of national purpose and unity needed to be strengthened by all possible means. The Party of Labour itself failed to gain a popular following for its program and disbanded in December 1918, some of its members joining the newly established Peasant Party (*Partid Țărănesc*). In any case, Brătianu's own bills won overwhelming approval in both the Chamber and the Senate, and on 19 July 1917 the King gave them his sanction.

In the meantime, Brătianu and his military commanders, on the advice of General Berthelot and his staff, had been feverishly engaged in reorganising and re-equipping the Romanian army to make it fit to resume large-scale operations. The task had not been easy. Units had to be rebuilt, often with new recruits and inexperienced officers; weapons and especially horses used for transport as well as the cavalry had to be replaced, and morale and a sense of mission restored. Berthelot's influence with the King and politicians continued to grow and was, on the whole, of much benefit. He saw to it that large numbers of machine-guns and artillery pieces and munitions of all kinds arrived from France and that a telegraph communications network between central command and units in the field, something utterly lacking in 1916, was put in place. By the early summer of 1917 a reasonably well-equipped army of some 460,000 men was ready to take the field.

Large-scale fighting on the Moldavian front resumed in July and August. Romanian forces under the command of General Averescu initiated the action on 22 July by launching an attack against Austro-Hungarian troops dug in near Mărăşti, in south-eastern Moldavia. The Romanian action was to be coordinated with a general Allied offensive on both the Russian and Western fronts, which was designed to deliver a crushing blow against the Central Powers and finally drive them from the War. The main task assigned to the Romanians was to hold down as many enemy troops as possible in order to prevent them from being transferred to other fronts. Averescu achieved some successes before being obliged to suspend operations. The victories of German and Austro-Hungarian armies against the Russians, notably their halting of General Lavr Kornilov's offensive in early July and their own counter-offensive, required the shifting of Russian troops from Moldavia to Galicia. The consequent weakening of the Moldavian front together with the collapse of morale among many Russian units persuaded Averescu of the need for caution.

The response of the Central Powers to the Romanian attack was not long in coming. Mackensen, the overall commander, launched a two-pronged offensive on 6 August near Mărăşeşti, just south of Mărăşti. Its purpose was to overwhelm Russian and Romanian units and force Romania to surrender, thereby opening the way to Odessa. The fighting lasted two weeks and was intense with heavy losses on both sides. But the Romanians held their ground. On 19 August Mackensen broke off his offensive after only modest advances.

The second prong of the offensive had begun on 8 August in the Oituz River Valley, northwest of Mărăşti; but it, too, failed to achieve any significant objective. Mackensen, obliged to transfer forces to the Italian front, finally halted operations on 3 September. Major fighting on the Moldavian front for 1917 thus came to an end. The Romanians could, however, claim a significant achievement: they had thwarted an all-out attempt by the Central Powers to force their withdrawal from the War.

Brătianu was also occupied with survival on the home front. The revolutionary events in Russia during the summer and early autumn filled him with apprehension. Along the Moldavian battle line public demonstrations by Russian soldiers, weary of war and aroused by the promises of a better life by the Bolsheviks and other radicals, and their invitations to Romanian soldiers and civilians to join them had created a volatile atmosphere hardly conducive to sustained military action. In the cities of Bacău and Târgu Ocna, near the front, Russian officers and soldiers had formed councils of deputies based on the model of the Petrograd Soviet which demanded immediate peace.

Also troubling for Brătianu was the emergence of a radical group of Romanian Social Democrats, who had been stirred by events in Russia and had committed themselves to bringing about similar drastic social and political changes in Romania. They denounced the War as a capitalist enterprise and praised the Revolution in Russia as the opening of a new era in the history of mankind, demanding that its benefits immediately be extended to Romania. Even though their numbers were small, Brătianu considered their activities destabilising and dangerous. In May and June his government tried to arrest their leaders. They fled to Odessa, where they carried on a relentless, if ineffective, propaganda campaign to overthrow 'Romanian Tsarism', though the revolution they had in mind was to be 'bourgeois-democratic', since they judged conditions in Romania still unsuited for a socialist revolution.[11] The Bolshevik Revolution in November changed their perception of things drastically, but brought them no closer to success.

Brătianu's already fragile relations with the Russian Provisional Government were further strained and the military situation in Moldavia made more complex by the movement for autonomy in Bessarabia led by Moldavian officers in the Russian army and intellectuals. Beginning in March 1917, when the first Russian Revolution brought down the Tsarist regime, Moldavians of all social classes began to demand an end to the old order in Bessarabia and its replacement by an autonomous Moldavian Republic. In early November, at the time of the Bolshevik Revolution, these efforts culminated in the convocation of a National Council, the Sfat al Țării, made up of 70 per cent Moldavians and the rest Russians, Bulgarians, Germans and Jews. After passionate debate the Council proclaimed the establishment of a Moldavian Democratic Federated Republic on 15 December and appealed to Romania to send troops to protect it from Bolshevik attacks. The Brătianu government in Iaşi, after an initial hesitation, sent a division to Chişinău, the capital, on 26 January 1918. Two weeks later, on 6 February, the Council declared the Moldavian Republic independent, an act which its Moldavian members regarded as merely a prelude to union with Romania.[12]

The prospect of recovering Bessarabia, under normal circumstances an occasion for celebration, was overshadowed by the success of the Bolsheviks in Petrograd. The consequences of their overthrow of the Provisional Government and of their determination to conclude a separate peace with the Central Powers as quickly as possible were all too clear to

Brătianu. Russia's withdrawal from the War would mean the disintegration of the battle front in Moldavia, as the Romanian army did not have the numbers or firepower necessary to resist the superior enemy forces it faced; it would also mean that Romania would be cut off from its sources of supplies in the West.

Faced with these realities, Brătianu came to the conclusion that Romania's military role in the War was over. He thought its contribution to the Allied war effort had been considerable because its army, by engaging large enemy forces, had relieved pressure on the Western Front and had thus made it possible for the Allies to withstand the German assault at Verdun in the latter months of 1916. In view of Romania's sacrifices on the field of battle, he saw no reason why its withdrawal from the conflict should invalidate the rewards it had been promised in its treaties of alliance with the Allies. To prepare Paris and London for the decision he thought unavoidable he gained the support of the French and British Ministers in Iaşi, Count Charles Saint-Aulaire and Sir George Barclay. Both accepted Brătianu's estimate that if the Romanian army were to carry on the struggle alone, it would be destroyed and thus could have no further influence on the outcome of the War. In a master stroke he even persuaded them and their Italian colleague to sign a statement on behalf of their respective governments authorising Romania to sign an armistice with the Central Powers and agreeing that it had fulfilled its treaty commitments to the Allies. The document had no validity since the Ministers had not been authorised by their respective governments to sign it, but Brătianu would use it later at the Paris Peace Conference as moral support for his demand that the Allies respect their commitments of 1916.

The reaction at home and abroad to Brătianu's decision

to leave the War was by no means entirely favourable. Take Ionescu and his party, who had joined Brătianu's Liberals in a national coalition government in July 1917 and were flatly opposed a separate peace with the Central Powers. Ionescu thought Brătianu erred in relying solely on the terms of the treaties with the Entente to achieve the Romanians' territorial ambitions. They must, he urged, continue to show their loyalty and their value as an ally by remaining actively engaged in the conflict. He thus shared the views of General Berthelot, who was adamantly opposed to Brătianu's policy and who had informed Georges Clemenceau, the French Prime Minister and Minister of War, that he had not been consulted by Brătianu and that, despite Brătianu's claims to the contrary, the Romanian army was prepared to carry on the struggle. Clemenceau reacted angrily to the news of a separate peace and threatened the Romanian government with reprisals. Although the incident was smoothed over, it proved to be only a prelude to the test of wills between the two men that unfolded over the next two years.

Events for the most part took the course Brătianu had foreseen. Although the Crown Council voted on 2 December to continue the struggle, Russia's decision to withdraw from the War proved decisive as it removed all serious resistance within the government to a separate peace. When the Russian commander on the Moldavian front, General Dmitry Shcherbachev, agreed to begin negotiations with Mackensen, the commander of German and Austro-Hungarian forces, for an armistice, Brătianu and his Cabinet concluded they had no other choice but to take part, if they hoped to preserve some measure of control over their country's future. The armistice of Brest-Litovsk signed by Russia and the Central Powers on 5 December brought hostilities on the Moldavian front to a formal end. But Romania's situation remained dire. Relations with the Bolshevik government deteriorated to the point where in late January 1918 the Council of Ministers in Petrograd broke diplomatic relations with Romania following Brătianu's instructions to Romanian army commanders to disarm and arrest Russian soldiers who committed violent acts and depradations.[13] At a meeting with Berthelot in early January Brătianu sought to justify the steps he was about to take by portraying Romania's situation in the most sombre terms. He pointed out that trains with provisions had stopped arriving, the Revolutionary government in Petrograd had in effect declared war on Romania and now, completely isolated, his government could expect no help from anyone, not even its Western allies who could offer only *sterile encouragements*.

Peace came slowly to the part of Romania that was still independent. Opposing armies remained in place, and Brătianu and the Liberals as well as other political formations could not bring themselves to sign a definitive peace. Under cover of the ceasefire concluded at Focşani with the Central Powers on 9 December Brătianu sought by every means to postpone the conclusion of a final peace. By February 1918 Mackensen had become so frustrated by Brătianu's tactics of delay that he issued an ultimatum to the Brătianu Cabinet requiring it to agree to a formal treaty within four days or face the resumption of hostilities. In this moment of crisis the coalition government of Liberals and Democratic Conservatives collapsed; Brătianu wanted to continue the armistice negotiations, whereas Take Ionescu demanded an immediate resumption of hostilities. They could agree on only one point: neither wanted to make peace with the Central Powers. Unable to govern and unwilling to yield to Mackensen's demands, Brătianu resigned on 8 February. The King, on his recommendation, entrusted the formation of a new government to General Averescu. He and Brătianu had agreed on the course before them. Averescu could see no alternative to a separate peace with the enemy, and Brătianu saw nothing to be gained by further resistance to overwhelming force. Yet, Brătianu did not despair of final victory by the Allies. Looking to the future and anxious to protect Romania's place at the peace conference, he urged Averescu to accept the terms set by the Central Powers unconditionally in order to show the Allies that Romania had had no choice but to accept an imposed peace.[14] Clemenceau and Lloyd George, when they were informed of Brătianu's plans, reacted angrily, and Lloyd George declared that the treaties with Romania would have to be revised.[15]

Decisive for the Romanian side was the conclusion of the Peace of Brest-Litovsk between Russia and the Central Powers on 3 March. Deprived of any last hope of Russian support and completely cut off from the Western Allies, the Averescu government signed the preliminary Peace of Buftea near Bucharest two days later. Its terms were harsh. In essence, it made Romania dependent politically and militarily on the Central Powers and subordinated its economy to their war effort. Yet, even now, Brătianu opposed a final peace agreement, probably in the expectation of Allied victory on the Western Front. Averescu, unable to cope without the support of the Liberals, resigned on 12 March and was succeeded as Prime Minister by Alexandru Marghiloman, a long-time leader of the Conservative Party who had remained in Bucharest when the government departed for Iaşi. He was a relative moderate who was intent on preserving the country's institutions, including the dynasty, and maintaining some semblance of independence. He was acceptable to the King and Brătianu because they hoped that his pro-German sympathies and his refusal to join the government in Iaşi would somehow soften the Central Powers' treatment of the country. Such hopes were illusory, as Germany and Austria-Hungary were determined to punish Romania for reneging on its treaty commitments in 1914 and took steps at once to gear its economy to their own war needs. The Treaty of Bucharest of 7 May, then, confirmed the provisions and intent of the Peace of Buftea by requiring the demobilisation of most of the Romanian army and by handing over control of the Romanian economy to Germany. Wallachia and Dobrudja remained under Central Power occupation, while Moldavia, more or less independent with its own administration, was almost completely cut off from the occupied areas.

Of immediate concern to Marghiloman was the ratification of the peace treaty. He had won a secure majority in Parliament in elections held in April from which the Liberals had abstained and gained approval of the Treaty of Bucharest. But he could not persuade the King to sign it, an obstinacy that reflected the widespread revulsion of both politicians and the public at the humiliating conditions imposed on the country and expressed their determination to resist, even if only by modest means.

The Marghiloman government, in addition to such pressing matters as agrarian reform and the maintenance of a delicate neutrality between the Central Powers and the Entente, had to deal with Bessarabia. It was a matter of utmost urgency as the outcome would influence relations with Bolshevik Russia and even affect the course of Romanian nation-building. Marghiloman had inherited the problem from the Brătianu government. In dealing with Bessarabia in the spring of 1918, Marghiloman for the most part simply followed the policy of the Liberals. He himself favoured the union of the province with Romania, and when the Sfat al Ţării declared for union on 27 March 1918 his government quickly accepted its decision.[16]

Events in the West in the summer and early autumn of 1918 largely determined the final outcome of Romania's war effort. The successes of Allied armies on the Western and Italian Fronts signalled the collapse of the Central Powers. In the Balkans the long-delayed Allied offensive from Salonica drove Bulgaria from the War on 30 September and the Ottoman Empire a month later. The Allied Army of the Danube, under the command of General Berthelot, who had left Romania after the Peace of Buftea, was poised to cross the Danube at Giurgiu at the end of October. On 3 November Austria-Hungary and on 11 November Germany accepted Allied terms for an Armistice.

In the meantime, Romanian leaders in Bukovina had taken advantage of Austria-Hungary's disintegration by forming on 27 October a National Council, which intended to seek union with Romania. When Ukrainian military forces occupied the capital Czernowitz (Cernăuţi) to prevent the incorporation of Ukrainian (Ruthenian) districts, the Council appealed to the Romanian government in Iaşi to send troops. The response was immediate. Romanian units forced the Ukrainians to withdraw and a few weeks later, on 28 November, the Council convoked a Romanian national congress, which overwhelmingly declared for union with Romania.

Brătianu and the Liberals were eager to re-enter the War on the side of the Allies as quickly as possible. They forced the Marghiloman government to resign on 6 November, and the King, at Brătianu's behest, appointed as Prime Minister General Constantin Coandă, who had served as the

Romanian army liaison at Russian military headquarters in 1916 and 1917. Brătianu's intention was to use the respite provided by the non-party Coandă government to prepare the way for the Liberals to return to power in full force. In any case, he, not Coandă, was in charge. He had three primary goals: the resumption of hostilities on the side of the Allies, the completion of agrarian and electoral reforms, and the consolidation of Greater Romania.

The King ordered his army to resume hostilities on 10 November. Although mobilisation had been hindered by the dispersal of officers and men after the Peace of Buftea and by the scarcity of weapons and equipment, some 90,000 troops were ready for the campaign by the middle of November, and units were already advancing from Moldavia toward Bucharest and into Dobrudja and Transylvania. German forces had begun to withdraw from occupied Romania on 10 November and by the end of the month all were across the Carpathians. On 1 December Ferdinand returned to his capital in triumph. On the same day an event of great symbolic importance was taking place beyond the mountains. At Alba Iulia representatives of the Romanians of Transylvania, the Banat and parts of eastern Hungary proclaimed their union with the Kingdom of Romania. Theirs was the final act in the territorial unification of Greater Romania.

Queen Marie of Romania arrives in Paris with her children, Princess Illeana and Prince Nicolas, 1920.

II

The Paris Peace Conference

6
Peace, 1919

Ionel Brătianu, his decision for war more than vindicated and his ideal of a united Romania all but fulfilled, arrived in Paris on 13 January 1919 to participate in the Peace Conference. As the Prime Minister he was the head of his country's delegation, which included his deputy, Nicolae Mişu, a long time political ally, his close advisers, General Constantin Coandă, Constantin Diamandy, Romanian Minister to Russia, Victor Antonescu, Romanian Minister to France and a representative each of the Romanians of Transylvania, the Banat, Bukovina and Bessarabia. But he knew that the burden of defending Romania's interests fell mainly to him. He thought it a solemn if not sacred responsibility, for the War, particularly the events of 1918, had seemed to him the culmination of a century-long struggle to bring into being a Romanian nation-state embracing all Romanians. Conscious of his place in history, he was thus determined to obtain all the territories and other benefits promised to him in the treaties of 1916. He wished to assert the rights of the modern ethnic state to full sovereignty and independence, protecting it from unwanted intrusions into its affairs by outsiders.

His ambitions ran counter to the broader aims of the Great Powers to establish a new international order and accomplish their own territorial and strategic purposes. Brătianu also faced the historical rivalries and the territorial claims of Romania's neighbours, both allies and enemies, in the first instance, Hungary and Russia, but also Serbia and Bulgaria.

Brătianu had first to convince the Big Three (Georges Clemenceau, David Lloyd George and Woodrow Wilson), especially the first two, that Romania should be admitted to the Conference as a full ally and be treated as an equal. He knew that Clemenceau and Lloyd George were dubious about Romania's status as an ally and its participation in the Conference. With victory assured, they no longer needed allies and argued that Romania, by signing the separate Peace of Buftea-Bucharest with the Central Powers, had annulled its rights to the rewards it had been promised. Brătianu rejected any such notion and maintained Romania's right to attend the Conference as an Allied Power.

Brătianu's relations with the three major allies, who with Italy and Japan constituted the Supreme Council, were unsurprisingly adversarial. The Council itself seemed eager to punish Romania for its capitulation in 1918, refusing to let Romania take part in the Conference as an equal, a stand that confirmed their general intention to reserve all final decisions to themselves, thereby relegating Romania to the ranks of states 'with limited interests'. But the Council went further: it allowed Romania only two official representatives at the Conference, while recognising the right of Serbia, which had not surrendered to the enemy, to have three. While the Council granted Romania representation on seven of the numerous Commissions formed to deal with specific issues it again seemed, in Brătianu's view, to go out of its way to disadvantage Romania by excluding its representatives from two Commissions that he considered crucial to the creation of a Romanian nation-state – those dealing with territorial boundaries and the status of minorities.

Among the Big Three, Brătianu found little understanding of Romania's aspirations to modern nationhood and even less sympathy for the means he himself was prepared to use to achieve it. His relations with Clemenceau, in particular, were never friendly as their personalities were incompatible and neither could bring himself to trust the other. Yet, certain similarities of character may also explain the dissonance between them. Both were stubborn and little given to compromise in matters they thought essential to the success of their cause. Clemenceau treated Brătianu brusquely and without the usual niceties Brătianu expected as head of government. He thought Brătianu something of a bore because of his tendency to turn his advocacy of the Romanian cause into a history lecture. For his part, Brătianu simply counted Clemenceau as an enemy of Romania. His correspondence during the Conference is filled with hostile references to the French Premier. But Clemenceau was not, in fact, a declared enemy of Romania. Rather, the attitude he assumed toward Brătianu's pleadings depended mainly on the situation of the moment and on how Brătianu's stance might affect the outcome of his own manoeuvrings. He and Brătianu had frequent meetings and despite personal and policy differences they understood the value of cooperation to achieve their respective aims.[1]

Brătianu counted much more on French than British or American support for Romania. His meetings with Lloyd George were decidedly cool; even over lunch they took the form of confrontations. They dealt mainly with Hungary, that is, Romania's territorial ambitions, the regime of Béla Kun, the Bolshevik threat to Eastern Europe and Romania's role as a bulwark against Bolshevism. Neither displayed friendly feelings toward the other, and at times they seemed to talk past one another. Brătianu was convinced that neither the Prime Minister nor the British in general had much understanding of European problems nor any desire to become deeply involved in its complex issues. Brătianu thought the British were satisfied with their gains from the War – the annexation of German colonies in Africa and the destruction of the German fleet – and would again concentrate their attention on their Empire and its commerce. In such a climate he had little hope of overcoming Lloyd George's vague disinterest in Romania's aspirations.[2]

Brătianu's differences with US President Woodrow Wilson were over matters of principle. Wilson came to the Peace Conference intent on creating a new international order that would enable nations to conduct relations with one another peacefully in a spirit of harmony and justice. Although he had advocated the right of peoples to self-determination in his Fourteen Points, he recognised the complexity of the issues involved. He was thus intent on setting in place the international machinery, first of all the League of Nations, necessary to moderate conflicting nationalist claims and promote compromise and cooperation. Brătianu, on the contrary, put the interests of the nation-state first. He was in Paris to receive international sanction of Greater Romania, that is, to obtain formal recognition of the union of Transylvania, the Banat, Bukovina and Bessarabia with the Kingdom of Romania. His negotiating model, as he himself admitted, was Machiavelli; and in the crucial debates over territory and minorities he almost always stood on the opposite side from Wilson's idealism. Wilson, in turn, regarded him as the representative of the old diplomacy, of the traditional international order.[3] But for Brătianu ideals were of little value unless sufficient force was available to put them into effect. His method of operating at the Conference, then, was to put his decisions into action and only afterwards find the principles necessary to justify them. Only then did Wilson's ideals become relevant for him.

Brătianu's intransigence made him thoroughly obnoxious to the Big Three. They were incensed by the challenges he continually raised to their authority on procedural as well as substantive issues. His use of threats and brinkmanship as a negotiating style sometimes brought his relations with his nominal allies to the breaking point. A striking case at the very opening of the Conference was his insistence that Romania's rights at the Conference as conferred by the 1916 Treaties could not be abrogated because of the separate peace with the Central Powers, since King Ferdinand had never sanctioned the Treaty of Bucharest. Brătianu then followed this declaration with a threat to withdraw from the Conference if he did not receive satisfaction.[4] The Big Three took such threats from a minor player with due self-restraint, but later when Brătianu's obstinacy in such crucial matters as the treatment of minorities and Romanian claims to Hungarian territory and the Romanian army's campaign in Hungary threatened to obstruct or delay unduly the course of peace-making, they responded menacingly.

While carrying on hard bargaining at the conference table and behind the scenes, Brătianu, the consummate politician, was keenly aware of the value of good public relations. He and his delegation did their utmost to win favour from a broader public and the press and from persons in high places

PRESIDENT WILSON'S FOURTEEN POINTS, 8 JANUARY 1918

The program of the world's peace, therefore, is our program; and that program, the only possible program, as we see it, is this:

I. Open covenants of peace, openly arrived at, after which there shall be no private international understandings of any kind but diplomacy shall proceed always frankly and in the public view.

II. Absolute freedom of navigation upon the seas, outside territorial waters, alike in peace and in war, except as the seas may be closed in whole or in part by international action for the enforcement of international covenants.

III. The removal, so far as possible, of all economic barriers and the establishment of an equality of trade conditions among all the nations consenting to the peace and associating themselves for its maintenance.

IV. Adequate guarantees given and taken that national armaments will be reduced to the lowest point consistent with domestic safety.

V. A free, open-minded, and absolutely impartial adjustment of all colonial claims, based upon a strict observance of the principle that in determining all such questions of sovereignty the interests of the populations concerned must have equal weight with the equitable claims of the government whose title is to be determined.

VI. The evacuation of all Russian territory and such a settlement of all questions affecting Russia as will secure the best and freest cooperation of the other nations of the world in obtaining for her an unhampered and unembarrassed opportunity for the independent determination of her own political development and national policy and assure her of a sincere welcome into the society of free nations under institutions of her own choosing; and, more than a welcome, assistance also of every kind that she may need and may herself desire. The treatment accorded Russia by her sister nations in the months to come will be the acid test of their good will, of their comprehension of her needs as distinguished from their own interests, and of their intelligent and unselfish sympathy.

VII. Belgium, the whole world will agree, must be evacuated and restored, without any attempt to limit the sovereignty which she enjoys in common with all other free nations. No other single act will serve as this will serve to restore confidence among the nations in the laws which they have themselves set and determined for the government of their relations with one another. Without this healing act the whole structure and validity of international law is forever impaired.

VIII. All French territory should be freed and the invaded portions restored, and the wrong done to France by Prussia in 1871 in the matter of Alsace-Lorraine, which has unsettled the peace of the world for nearly fifty years, should be righted, in order that peace may once more be made secure in the interest of all.

IX. A readjustment of the frontiers of Italy should be effected along clearly recognizable lines of nationality.

X. The peoples of Austria-Hungary, whose place among the nations we wish to see safeguarded and assured, should be accorded the freest opportunity to autonomous development.

XI. Rumania, Serbia, and Montenegro should be evacuated; occupied territories restored; Serbia accorded free and secure access to the sea; and the relations of the several Balkan states to one another determined by friendly counsel along historically established lines of allegiance and nationality; and international guarantees of the political and economic independence and territorial integrity of the several Balkan states should be entered into.

XII. The Turkish portion of the present Ottoman Empire should be assured a secure sovereignty, but the other nationalities which are now under Turkish rule should be assured an undoubted security of life and an absolutely unmolested opportunity of autonomous development, and the Dardanelles should be permanently opened as a free passage to the ships and commerce of all nations under international guarantees.

XIII. An independent Polish state should be erected which should include the territories inhabited by indisputably Polish populations, which should be assured a free and secure access to the sea, and whose political and economic independence and territorial integrity should be guaranteed by international covenant.

XIV. A general association of nations must be formed under specific covenants for the purpose of affording mutual guarantees of political independence and territorial integrity to great and small states alike.

in Paris and other European capitals who might be persuaded to lend the Romanian cause their good will. Brătianu himself could be charming when the mood suited him, but too often his sociability gave way to partisan advocacy for his cause. He acknowledged that he needed help in swaying minds and hearts. He found it in Queen Marie.

Marie came to Paris in March 1919 for the express purpose of serving her adopted country as an ambassador of good will. Brătianu fully approved because he was well aware of how valuable her personal contacts with royalty and the elites in France and Britain could be and how the esteem in which she was held because of her work with the Red Cross and her numerous visits to the battlefield during the campaigns of 1916 and 1917 might influence negotiations at the Conference. He had already called on her shortly after Romania's entry into the War to help the cause by corresponding with her relatives at both the British and Russian courts, namely King George V and Tsar Nicholas II. Then, after the War as she embarked on a personal mission to Western capitals, he was careful to associate her with his own aims in Paris. Thus, before meeting Clemenceau he went over with her in detail the issues that she was to raise.[5]

Marie was indeed treated as a celebrity almost everywhere (though Clemenceau seems to have been unimpressed) and she made the ritual rounds of official visits and held the obligatory press conferences, all of which she bore with equanimity and for the most part with genuine satisfaction, as unlike Brătianu she was very much a public person. Despite marked differences in personality, the Queen and the Prime Minister got on well and worked together smoothly in presenting the Romanian cause to official audiences that knew little of the country's history and cared even less about its aspirations.

Brătianu praised her work in Paris and London, confessing that she had accomplished more in a few days than his Ambassadors had been able to do in a month. He even attributed a slight softening of Clemenceau's and Lloyd George's attitude toward Romania to her good works. For her part, Marie found Brătianu eager to preach and little interested in a genuine exchange of views, probably the reason why Clemenceau, as he confided to her, found Brătianu's behaviour off putting. But she also praised his devotion to Romania and acknowledged that he could be 'very congenial company'. In London in the latter part of March they worked together to modify the generally unfavourable attitude of British officials toward Romania. Marie arranged a lunch between Brătianu and King George V, at which 'Brătianu displayed all his charm' and at which she had to serve as translator in order 'to keep the conversation afloat', since the King was not very fluent in French. On the whole, Marie thought Brătianu was satisfied with the results of their short visit to London and 'seemed less worried than before'.

Of the many issues that soured relations between Brătianu and the Big Three, Brătianu's long-standing resentment of the Great Powers for what he perceived to be their arrogance in dealing with smaller states was ever present. His attitude stemmed from his earlier dealings with them as Foreign Minister and Prime Minister and to his extensive reading of Romanian and European history. Now, in Paris, he found confirmation of his feelings in the disdainful treatment accorded him and his cause. Entertaining little hope of influencing the behaviour of French and British statesmen whom he regarded as the prime movers of Conference business, he had turned to Wilson, whose advocacy of the self-determination of small nations and of a new era of openness in international relations suggested the possibility of change in Great Power-Small Power relations. But he found Wilson little moved by his arguments. In a general debate over the provisions of the Minorities Treaty in May, he accused the Supreme Council of imposing its own solutions on all the problems raised by the War, even demanding the right to intervene in the political and economic affairs of smaller states without recognising their right to have a voice in such matters. Mincing no words, he declared it *America's duty to guarantee the security of those nations whose frontiers and internal political organisation Wilson was seeking to reconfigure, even to the detriment of their well-being*.[6] But his rebukes and pleadings were without effect, the lines drawn between the Great and Small Powers seeming to him as rigid as ever. The notion of states 'with general interests' (the Great) opposed to those 'with limited interests' (the Small) was, he thought, dangerous for the latter since they were in effect being treated as states with limited independence.

> '[It is] America's duty to guarantee the security of those nations whose frontiers and internal political organisation Wilson was seeking to reconfigure, even to the detriment of their well-being.'
>
> **ION BRĂTIANU**

Repeatedly unsuccessful in direct approaches to the Big Three, Brătianu now tried to create a common front of small East European victor nations (Czechoslovakia, Poland, Serbia and Greece along with Romania) in order to impress upon the Powers the need for a more sympathetic hearing of their grievances. In May the issue he (and they) chose for a test of strength was the proposed treaty with Austria. They were particularly exasperated by the refusal of the Powers to show them the draft of the treaty before it was handed to the

Austrian delegates, thus depriving them of the opportunity to propose changes. Although Brătianu and his colleagues gained a 48-hour delay before the treaty's presentation to the Austrians, their intervention had no effect on its content.

It was in such a strained atmosphere that Brătianu pursued his main objective at the Conference: the securing of the boundaries of the Greater Romania that had come into being almost spontaneously in the preceding year. He was blunt and uncompromising and thus reinforced the perception of him by the Big Three and others that he was an obstacle to normal peacemaking and should thus expect no favours. For his part, Brătianu was convinced that the territories he coveted should not be thought of as concessions or marks of generosity on the part of the Powers. Rather, he argued, they belonged to Romania by right, as confirmed not only by treaty and by history but also by sacrifices on the field of battle.

Early in the Conference proceedings he came before the Supreme Council twice as it deliberated territorial questions. Before making his first appearance on 31 January to present Romania's case, Clemenceau asked him not to raise the matter of the Treaties of 1916 in order to avoid upsetting Wilson. Brătianu ignored the suggestion and launched into an extended exposition of Romania's rights as guaranteed by the Treaties. Determined to get all he thought Romania was due, he flatly rejected any compromise on its territorial claims. He made a particular issue of the Banat as somehow illustrative of what was at stake between Romania and the Powers. He demanded the cession of the entire Banat in accordance with the Treaty of 1916, and he cited both history (he claimed that the ancestors of the Romanians were the first to settle the area) and statistics on ethnicity (the Romanians were the largest nationality in the region as a whole) to buttress his arguments. He adamantly opposed partition, even though he could not deny that the western third of the Banat was inhabited mainly by Serbs, because, he warned, partition would destroy the region's 'economic and political integrity'. He also appealed to his listeners' sense of justice by citing the deaths of over 300,000 Romanian soldiers in the War as reason enough to honour Romania's claims. But they were unmoved. On the following day he continued his exposition, adding the argument that Romania should receive all the territory promised in 1916 because it had supported the cause of the Entente to the utmost of its capabilities. He would have none of the proposal from Council members that plebiscites in the disputed territories (Bukovina, Transylvania and Bessarabia) conducted by independent bodies would provide a better gauge of public sentiment there than the national assemblies that had declared for union with Romania in the chaotic conditions of the previous year. Although he admitted the Hungarians of Transylvania would certainly vote against union with Romania, since they were opposed to becoming a mere minority under a people they had ruled for a thousand years, he promised that Romania would grant the Hungarians and all other minorities full rights of citizenship.[7] But his pleas and exhortations were to no avail. The Council withheld approval of Romania's territorial acquisitions and agreed only to establish a Romanian Territorial Commission, whose function would be to investigate Romanian claims and judge their legitimacy.[8] The Commission, meeting for the first time on 8 February and influenced mainly by its American, British and French members, made its report to the Central Territorial Commission on 6 April. It was sympathetic to the Romanian position, recommending frontiers that placed most of what came to be known as Transylvania, including a large part of the Banat, within the new Romania. But the Commission also took note of the substantial minority populations in the territory that would thus come under Romanian administration and urged that their rights be formally guaranteed. The Council of Four (Clemenceau, Lloyd George, Wilson and Orlando of Italy) approved the report on 12 May.

Of all the territorial issues that arose between Brătianu and the Supreme Council, the new frontier to be drawn between Romania and Hungary was the most contentious. Gaining possession of Transylvania was Brătianu's paramount objective for both strategic and emotional reasons. He recognised the province as crucial to the security of the new Romania, both militarily and economically, and he accepted without question the historical dogma fashioned in the latter 18th and early 19th century that it had been the birthplace of the Romanian nation. Hardly a Romanian could be found to dispute this thesis. At the Conference, then, he pushed the boundaries of Transylvania as far to the west as possible, to the Tisza River, as the most appropriate line of defence. But he found it impossible to manage the acquisition of Transylvania as a simple, straightforward transaction. It became entangled in a maze of other, more sweeping issues: the intention of the Big Three to set the general conditions of peace and lay the foundations of a new international order in accordance with their own best interests; the future of minority populations in the newly formed or enlarged states of Central and South-eastern Europe, in Romania in particular; and the need to counteract the threat of Bolshevism in the same region.

On the matter of Hungary, Brătianu and the Romanian army took the initiative between November 1918 and August 1919. They repeatedly ignored the express wishes, even commands, of the Supreme Council by in effect calling its bluff at critical moments. One issue continually in dispute had to do with limiting the Romanian army's advance into Transylvania until the Council had reached decisions on territorial boundaries. General Franchet d'Esperey, commander of all Allied forces in South-eastern Europe, had drawn a demarcation line between the Hungarian and Romanian armies on 13 November 1918 which followed the Mureş River in central Transylvania. It had not held. Romanian troops continued their advance westward against feeble Hungarian resistance, despite the order of the Council on 25 January 1919 to halt. By this time the Romanian army had pushed beyond Kolozsvár (Cluj) on a broad front half-way to Nagyvárad (Oradea). Further efforts by the Inter-Allied War Council in Paris to bring hostilities to an end by tracing a new demarcation line between Romanian and Hungarian troops on 25 February brought only a temporary lull. The Supreme Council approved the new line, which ran from Szatmár (Satu Mare) in the north near Nagyvárad to Arad in the south and left all three important cities on the Hungarian side. As a further guarantee of a ceasefire it created a neutral zone just to the west of the demarcation line. This initiative, taken in the interests of peace and stability, had consequences that no one had foreseen. It provoked an impassioned protest from the Hungarian government headed by the Prime Minister and then President since the previous October, Mihály Károlyi, who pointed out that the new boundary took from Hungary territory inhabited overwhelmingly by Hungarians. When the Council remained firm in its decision, Károlyi, faced with mounting opposition to his government over the general course of events and feeling himself unable to master the situation, resigned on 20 March. He was replaced as Prime Minister by the Communist Béla Kun, who formed a new government composed of Communists and left wing Socialists and immediately, on 21 March, proclaimed Hungary a Soviet Republic.

Events in Budapest were a godsend for Brătianu; it gave him a magnificent opportunity to press his case for his army's further advance into Hungary, as he had become acutely aware of the Allies' apprehensions about the spread of Bolshevism into Central Europe. He had recently spent a week in London trying to soften British attitudes toward him and his cause. Now, back in Paris, he had lunch with Lloyd George on 25 March. He used the occasion to bring up the 'Bolshevik menace' again and urged him to maintain a united front of all the Allies, large and small, to combat it. Specifically, he proposed the immediate sending of significant Allied military aid to the Poles and the Romanians, who were, he pointed out, on the frontiers of Revolutionary Russia, to enable them to hold back the tide of Bolshevism. He had already engaged in an intense lobbying campaign against the Hungarian Soviet Republic and was anxious to gain authorisation from the Supreme Council for a deeper thrust into Hungary. He was certain the Big Three would not hesitate to reward Romania with territorial concessions along its western borders if it contributed to the overthrow of Béla Kun's government.

Brătianu's expectations of close cooperation with the Council in an anti-Bolshevik crusade were, however, undone when its members decided to seek an understanding with Kun by sending an emissary, General Jan Christian Smuts of South Africa whom Lloyd George had recently appointed Minister without Portfolio, to Budapest in early April. Brătianu's great fear was that a reconciliation might indeed take place and as a consequence the Council would recognise the Soviet Republic and invite it to send delegates to the Peace Conference. If this happened, then he was certain his task would become more difficult. But as matters turned out, he had little reason to worry. Kun was not at all in a conciliatory mood and rather than discussing ways of reaching an agreement, he bluntly rejected the authority of the Council to draw political boundaries for Hungary. Instead, he demanded that it reinstate the old demarcation line along the Mureş River of the previous November and force the Romanian army to respect it. Utterly stymied, Smuts returned to Paris on 12 April.

By this time Brătianu in Paris and his Council of Ministers in Bucharest had already agreed on an independent course of action. They were determined not to yield the initiative to the Council on a matter they judged critical to the future of Romania. On 10 April they decided to send the army deeper into Hungary.[9] A minor attack by Hungarian forces in the area of the Munţii Apuseni in western Transylvania on the night of 15/16 April gave Romanian operations the appearance of a counter-attack, thereby providing cover from accusations by the Council that Brătianu was using the whole episode as a pretext to pursue his territorial ambitions. Brătianu's main objective was to establish the Tisza River, at least the southern part where the Mureş flowed into it, as the western frontier of Romania. He made no secret of his plans. In a memorandum to Wilson on 22 April he confessed he wanted to create borders secure enough to enable the Romanians to live in peace and to develop their economy to the fullest. Nonetheless, he had doubts about the wisdom of marching on to Budapest. It might not be in Romania's interest, he reasoned, to remove the Bolsheviks, since the Soviet Republic, weak and chaotic, might be succeeded by a more stable regime better able to win Allied support and thus thwart his designs on Hungarian territory. In any case, as he informed his colleagues in Bucharest on 25 April, he was not going to allow *political difficulties*, by which he meant censure from the Supreme Council, to stand in the way.[10] The Romanian army's advance met little serious resistance, and by early May it had penetrated deeply into eastern Hungary.

By this time relations between Brătianu and the Supreme Council were close to a rupture. On 10 June the Council severely rebuked him for his refusal to respect Franchet d'Esperey's demarcation line of the previous November and suggested that his actions were ultimately the cause of the governmental crisis in Hungary that had led to Károlyi's resignation and had brought Kun and the Bolsheviks to power, and it was little disposed to negotiate further with Brătianu on the matter as it was faced with a new complication: the assault of the Hungarian Red Army on Slovakia on 30 May. But Kun, unexpectedly, responded in a conciliatory way to the Council's ultimatum that he cease military operations. Wishing to settle territorial issues between Hungary and Romania, the Council now demanded that Brătianu order his forces to withdraw from the Tisza to the demarcation line established in February. But he remained inflexible, insisting that to do so would deprive the Romanian army of its only viable defensive position. When he reminded the Council that he was not responsible for social conditions in Hungary, the Council warned him that unless he complied it would cut off all aid to Romania. As neither side was willing to compromise, each went its own way. On 11 June, the Advisory Council of Foreign Ministers informed the Romanian delegation that it had drawn new frontiers for their country, a decision confirmed the following day by the Council of Four, which had taken the place of the Supreme Council.

At the same time that territorial questions were bringing

relations between Brătianu and the Supreme Council to an impasse, the two sides were embroiled in an equally acrimonious dispute over the rights of minorities in post-war Romania. The main issue was essentially the same as it had been in 1878 – the civil status of Romanian Jews. Just as at the Congress of Berlin the Powers had imposed their own solution in the face of strong Romanian resistance, the Powers proceeded in the same way now at Paris. They inserted an article in the treaty with Austria that required the Romanian government to assure equal rights to Jews and in future to take other measures that the principal Allies might deem necessary to fulfil its obligations. They also planned to put these provisions in a general Minorities Treaty, which Romania (and other countries) would be invited to sign. Jewish organisations in Western Europe had used their considerable influence to gain these Great Power guarantees for any promises the Romanian government might make to end the discriminatory treatment of Jews.

Brătianu objected strenuously. His arguments were similar to those he had raised with Luigi Luzzatti in 1913. He pointed out, first, that Romania's sovereignty would be undermined if it were to allow foreign states to intervene in its internal affairs; and, second, that its political unity would be undone, if it were to recognise the existence of ethnic minority 'enclaves' within its borders. He put his case succinctly at a session of the Supreme Council on 31 May. First of all, he argued that the proposed guarantees in the Austrian treaty were unnecessary as his government had already assured all citizens of equality of rights and of political and religious liberties. He emphasised that these guarantees specifically included the inhabitants of the newly acquired territories, and he promised that laws already in force would be supplemented by an extensive

administrative decentralisation aimed at ensuring populations of different ethnic origins the unfettered development
of language, education and culture and the free exercise of
religion. In any case, he thought it the primary responsibility
of a sovereign state like Romania to ensure the liberties and
equal treatment of all its citizens and in this way contribute
to the harmonising of relations between the different ethnic
communities. Foreign intervention, he feared, would have the
opposite effect since it would encourage minorities to seek
protection and a redress of grievances outside the country in
which they lived. Foreign intervention, he reiterated, would
create a two-tier system of citizenship that would eventually
destabilise the new state.[11]

When Clemenceau, who was presiding at the session, suggested that 'more complete' guarantees than those noted by
Brătianu might be necessary, he could not help recalling the
long history of complaints from Jewish citizens about the
failure of Romanian governments, both Liberal and Conservative, to carry out promises made at the Congress of Berlin
in 1878. But, in an unusually conciliatory gesture, he tried to
reassure Brătianu that the Powers had no wish to intervene in
Romania's affairs, let alone diminish its sovereignty. Rather,
he pointed out that the monitoring of Romania's treatment
of minorities would be done by the League of Nations, whose
rules would apply to all states great and small. Brătianu, who
had apparently received the text of the Treaty only 24 hours
earlier, was quick to call attention to an inconsistency in Clemenceau's interpretation of the article concerning minorities.
Since it granted the Great Powers the right to take measures
they thought necessary to safeguard the rights of minorities,
Brătianu argued that it was, in fact, they, not the League of
Nations, who would intervene in Romania's internal affairs.

Clemenceau conceded the point, but he thought Brătianu and his colleagues could not object to receiving 'friendly counsel' from their friends. But Brătianu would not be mollified. He insisted that what the Supreme Council was, in effect, proposing was not friendly advice at all but rather a formal engagement that would permit foreign states to decide on matters crucial to the existence of another state. How, he wondered, could minorities who looked to foreign states to guarantee their liberties not in time compromise the integrity of the state whose citizens they were?

Brătianu continued his polemic with the members of the Council in writing. Especially revealing of his views on the minorities question was the letter he addressed to Wilson on 6 June. He came right to the point on what seemed to him the crux of the matter: the Jewish question. He wanted Wilson and the other members of the Big Four to understand that the issue before them had nothing to do with religious toleration. It was rather a purely social and economic question caused, in his view, by the immigration of Jews into the Romanian lands particularly in rural areas which could not support a massive influx of foreigners whose style of life and ways of doing business undermined stability in the villages. Legislation, he insisted, had been necessary to remedy the situation. But now, he pointed out, the Jewish question as raised at the Peace Conference had been resolved by a decree-law promulgated by his government in May providing for the naturalisation of Jews. But it did not address the issue before the Council: enforcement of the promises made to the minorities.

Brătianu was adamant in his refusal to modify his stand on the minorities and territorial issues. His strained relations with the Council and his feeling of being treated as an enemy or one of the defeated powers led him to leave Paris for Bucharest on 2 July, just a few days after he had signed the Treaty of Versailles on 28 June. Despite heavy pressure from the Allies, he stoutly refused to sign the Treaty with Austria as long as the articles on minorities remained in place. Consequently, when the formal signing of the Treaty of St Germain took place on 10 September, no Romanian delegate was present. Two days later Brătianu and his Cabinet resigned, citing as reasons the Allies' disregard of their Treaty commitments of 1916 and their persistence in imposing conditions on Romania incompatible with its sovereignty. Brătianu's Minister of War, General Arthur Văitoianu, succeeded him on 29 September, but no one doubted who exercised the power of decision behind the scenes. Brătianu expected the Văitoianu government to keep the Liberal administrative apparatus fully intact and to make preparations for national elections, which he had no doubt the Liberal Party would win by a wide margin. Such a ringing endorsement of his policies from the Romanian public would, he was certain, strengthen his hand immeasurably in dealing with his tormentors in Paris.

Yet, after returning home all had not gone his way. Strong opposition to his policy of intransigence in Paris came from his rival and occasional colleague Take Ionescu. The press affiliated with his Nationalist-Conservative Party, as it was now called, sharply criticised Brătianu's tactics as having created a hostile environment for Romania at the Peace Conference and accused him, as a result, of failing to defend the country's vital interests. The recently formed League of the People (*Liga Poporului*), led by Alexandru Averescu, also objected to a foreign policy of go-it-alone and confrontation with allies. Even Brătianu's own efforts to respond to these attacks and to counteract growing opposition to the Liberals in the Old Kingdom failed; his offer to the Romanian

National Party of Transylvania to form a broad coalition was rejected.

Of all the issues Brătianu had had to face, it was the Romanian-Hungarian boundary dispute and the advance of the Romanian army into Hungary that had brought relations between the Supreme Council and the Romanian government closest to an open break and which did most to undo his political calculations at home. In Bucharest he showed no more willingness to compromise than he had in Paris. Romanian troops responded to a Hungarian attack on 20 July by marching to Budapest, which they entered on 3 August. Two days earlier the Communist government had dissolved itself, and Béla Kun and many of his associates had fled into exile. The Romanian army's occupation of Budapest, its large-scale requisitioning of goods of all kinds and its attempts to impose an armistice on the new Hungarian government, all in defiance of repeated protests and threats from the Supreme Council, led the principal Allies on 15 November to send a final ultimatum to Bucharest. It demanded that within eight days the Văitoianu government withdraw its troops from Hungary to the border specified by the Peace Conference, cease all requisitioning of goods in Hungary, cooperate with an inter-Allied Commission to estimate the value of goods already taken and sign the Austrian and Minorities Treaties. After receiving a short extension of time to comply, the government rejected the terms of the ultimatum and on 30 November resigned.[12] Văitoianu was simply carrying out Brătianu's instructions. Brătianu himself was convinced that Romania had a right to seize goods from Hungary as compensation for the far larger quantities of goods taken by German and Austro-Hungarian armies during their occupation of Romania, and he was anxious to postpone for as long as possible the withdrawal of Romanian troops from the 'natural defence line' of the Tisza River. As for the Austrian and the Minorities Treaties, he continued to regard them as incompatible with national sovereignty, and thus no government he controlled would sign them.

Certain changes in the negotiating style of the Romanian government occurred as Văitoianu was succeeded by the Transylvanian Alexandru Vaida on 1 December 1919 at the head of the so-called Parliamentary Bloc government, composed of a number of parties including the Romanian National Party, all united by their opposition to the Liberals. Whereas Brătianu was antagonistic and determined to put off agreements until the last possible concession had been wrung out, Vaida was conciliatory and willing to sign the Treaties first and then negotiate modifications. It was Vaida, in fact, who obtained significant changes in the Austrian and Minorities Treaties, notably the elimination of articles containing specific references to Romanian Jews. Vaida accepted the new terms. He and his colleagues and indeed the great majority of Romanian politicians wanted to re-establish good relations with the Western Powers, which they knew were essential for the smooth development of the new Romania. Vaida also agreed in principle to settle issues with Hungary in accordance with the wishes of the Allies, although all sides were certain that controversy and further negotiations were inevitable. As a result, he sent General Constantin Coandă, now Secretary General in the Ministry of War, to Paris as Romania's delegate to the Peace Conference. It was Coandă who signed the Austrian and the Minorities Treaties on 10 December.

The Supreme Council and its successor, the Council of Ambassadors, now moved to approve new boundaries between Romania and its neighbours. Issues between Romania and

Bulgaria were quickly disposed of, as the Treaty of Neuilly of 27 November 1919 between the Allies and Bulgaria left intact the frontier established in the Dobrudja by the Treaty of Bucharest in 1913. The dispute between Romania and the new Yugoslav state over the Banat was also settled with relative ease. Brătianu had wanted all of it, but the Supreme Council drew boundaries largely along ethnic lines, which gave Romania two-thirds of the territory and Yugoslavia the rest.

An accord on Romania's acquisition of Bessarabia had proved difficult from the very beginning of the Peace Conference and had engaged Brătianu's powers of negotiation to the fullest. He argued his case passionately. He insisted that the Sfat al Țării, which declared union with Romania, was a legal assembly; and he claimed that the Dniester River, the eastern boundary of Bessarabia, must be the frontier of the new Romania because Bessarabia in the hands of others (he of course meant Soviet Russia) would constitute a mortal threat to Romania's very existence. The Allies were little moved by such emotion and still less inclined to seek a quick solution of the problem. They eventually linked the fate of Bessarabia to the Romanian-Hungarian boundary dispute and thus the matter dragged on until 1920. The Council of Ambassadors, which had as its main responsibility the tidying-up of loose ends, would not sign the treaty on Bessarabia that it had itself drawn up until Romania had reached a final settlement with Hungary over boundaries and other matters raised by the Romanian occupation. Finally, that obstacle was removed by the signing of the Treaty of Trianon on 4 June 1920, which awarded Romania most of what Brătianu had sought: all of historical Transylvania and a part of eastern Hungary, including the largely Hungarian cities of Nagyvárad and Arad.

It was only on 28 October that the Council of Ambassadors presented the Romanian government, now headed by
General Alexandru Averescu who had succeeded Vaida on 13
March 1920, with a treaty on the union of Bessarabia with
Romania. It recognised Romanian sovereignty over the area
between the Prut and Dniester Rivers and specified the Dniester as the new boundary between Romania and Bolshevik
Russia. The Ambassadors acknowledged that Russia had not
been a party to the negotiations, but they urged it to observe
the treaty's provisions until such time as a government was in
place with which the Allies could carry on normal relations.
They also promised that the Council of the League Nations
would arbitrate matters in dispute, but they left a settlement
of specific issues to direct negotiations between Romania and
Russia. The two sides, in fact, never reached a meeting of the
minds on matters in dispute. Thus, Bessarabia remained a
major source of friction, as the Soviet Union refused to recognise Romanian possession of the territory, even after the
two countries had established diplomatic relations in 1934.

By the autumn of 1920 the Romania envisioned by Ionel
Brătianu had largely come into being. The acquisition of
the new provinces had gained international sanction and
had more than doubled the territory of pre-war Romania to
296,000 square kilometres and had nearly doubled its population to 16,250,000 in 1919. The great majority of Romanians
were now within the boundaries of the national state, but
the fulfilment of this long-held aspiration had added substantial minorities. Before the War the minority population had
been roughly 8 per cent of the total population, but now it
had increased to over 25 per cent: Hungarians (9.3 per cent)
were the largest, followed by Jews (5.3 per cent), Ukrainians
(4.7 per cent) and Germans (4.3 per cent). The new territories

and the new populations added enormously to the country's productive capabilities, especially its industrial capacity, for which Transylvania and the Banat were mainly responsible.

All of these gains had been made at the cost of substantial human and material losses. Some 300,000 soldiers had been killed in battle, and when they are added to the deaths of civilians the total reaches roughly one-tenth of the country's pre-war population. All branches of the economy, agriculture as well as industry, commerce and transportation, had suffered incalculable damage. Production had fallen dramatically to less than half, in some cases, a fifth, of pre-war output. For example, oil was at 47 per cent, coal at 41 per cent and metallurgy at 19.4 per cent. In agriculture, because of the lack of adequate labour, tools and machinery, the country, a large exporter of agricultural products before the War, had to import food to satisfy the urgent needs of the population.[13]

Brătianu saw formidable tasks ahead. He knew that building Greater Romania had just begun. First of all, the damage of war, moral as well as material, had to be repaired. Then, the new territories with their diverse ethnicities, religions and historical traditions and their multiplicity of institutions and identities had somehow to be integrated into existing structures. Only then could he contemplate focusing his energies on the pursuit of his long-held ideal of Romania as a modern state and society.

7

Greater Romania, 1919–1927

A new Liberal government headed by Ionel Brătianu had, as we have seen, been installed in November 1918 and had proceeded at once to fulfil the promises of agrarian and electoral reform made during the War. But politically Brătianu had had a sense that all was not well and had postponed elections for a year. The hardships of the War, the wrangling with allies at Paris, and the uncertainties of the transition from war to recovery had made large segments of the population restless, and political parties based in the newly acquired provinces or arising out of the peasantry and its defenders posed a threat to Liberal predominance. Brătianu had finally yielded to pressure from the activist public and his political rivals and scheduled parliamentary elections for November 1919, fully confident his party would be able to manage them in the usual way. But he and his colleagues had miscalculated. Their party gained only 22 per cent of the vote and only 103 deputies out of 568. Thus, for the first time the party in control of the government administrative machinery had failed to obtain an absolute majority of seats in the Chamber of Deputies. The Romanian National Party, mainly Transylvanian, with 119

Europe 1923

FINLAND

Petrograd (St Petersburg)

Tallinn
ESTONIA

Riga
LATVIA

LITHUANIA

Vilnius

önigsberg
T
SIA

Moscow

UNION OF SOVIET
SOCIALIST REPUBLICS

Varsaw   Brest-Litovsk

POLAND

Kiev

est

Odessa

ROMANIA

Bucharest

Black Sea

BULGARIA
Sofia

Istanbul

GREECE

TURKEY

Athens

IRAQ

SYRIA

CYPRUS

seats and the new Peasant Party with 61 seats were the chief beneficiaries of universal suffrage as many voters looked to new parties and new people to solve pressing social and economic problems. One long-time force in Romanian political life was absent. The Conservative Party, its chief source of strength the large landholders, undermined by post-war land redistribution and its patriotism questioned because of the pro-German sentiments of many of its leaders, had simply disintegrated.[1]

On 1 December 1919, a coalition led by the Romanian National Party formed the so-called Parliamentary Bloc government with Alexandru Vaida as Prime Minister. Its political and economic program was democratic, and its way of doing business represented an advance on Liberal practice. As we have seen, it strove to repair relations with the Allies by signing the Austrian and Minorities Treaties on 10 December. But its tenure was short-lived as the reforms it promoted aroused bitter opposition from Liberals and others outside the Bloc (and even within the Bloc), and its lack of unity and a master plan for social and economic reform left it weakened.

Brătianu was intent on returning to power, but for the moment he was willing to proceed slowly in a period of disarray if only to persuade public opinion that the Liberals alone could ensure order and an effective government. Convinced that the Bloc was too loosely structured to cope with either domestic or foreign challenges and worried by the radical nature of the reforms being pushed by the Peasant Party, he persuaded the King to replace the Bloc government with one headed by Alexandru Averescu. He had already come to an understanding with the popular war hero on legislation to bring about moderate agrarian reform and revive the national economy. King Ferdinand followed Brătianu's advice and entrusted the formation of a new government to Averescu on 13 March 1920.

Harmony between the new Prime Minister and Brătianu quickly dissolved. Brătianu had assumed that Averescu would pursue Liberal policies until he, Brătianu, had decided that the time was right to return to power. But Averescu, ignoring Liberal economic interests, showed a surprising independence and seemed to be preparing the ground for a long tenure. Brătianu, incensed, organised a campaign to unseat him that won over almost the entire opposition and, most importantly, the King.

Brătianu became Prime Minister again in January 1922 and remained the head of a powerful Liberal government until August 1926. Even during the brief tenures of the Parliamentary Bloc and Averescu governments he had remained the most important political figure in the country. Now, once again in control of all the levers of power, he was determined to proceed with his ambitious plan to transform old Romania into a fully European state. His main goals remained the same: to consolidate Greater Romania as a unitary national state, to modernise the foundations of its economy, to mobilise its educational and cultural resources and to ensure the security of its expanded borders.

Yet, in early 1920s Romania little had changed since the turn of the century. On the one hand, underdevelopment persisted as largely traditional agriculture remained the foundation of the national economy. The great majority of the population, 78 per cent of some 16 million inhabitants, lived in the countryside and depended on agriculture as their primary source of income. But the productivity of agriculture and the prosperity of peasants were constantly imperilled by an organisation and a technology that did not differ significantly from that which had prevailed in the latter decades of the 19th century. Romania also remained bound to the West as the main purchaser of its agricultural goods, the major supplier of manufactures and the primary source of investments and loans.

Yet, there was change. Industry was growing, in some branches such as metallurgy and oil impressively so, and even in agriculture the long reliance on grains was slowly yielding to vegetable and industrial crops. Subtle shifts were also discernible in the social structure as urbanisation, spurred by industrialisation and a steady migration from the countryside to cities, took place. Yet, for Brătianu, the economic and social change was too slow and haphazard. He was certain sustained progress required the constant stimulus and coordination that only a strong central government and a dynamic political party could provide.

To accomplish his grand design of making Romania an integral part of Europe, Brătianu wanted first to bring the machinery of government under his full control. His instrument for doing so was, not surprisingly, the Liberal Party which he continued to think of as a truly national party, committed to promoting the general welfare of all sections of society. For Brătianu, the Liberal Party stood for progress and he could point to the agrarian and electoral reforms and the territorial unification that he and his fellow Liberals had championed since the beginning of the century.

Yet, despite Brătianu's claims, the Liberal Party was, in fact, a class party, its policies and ambitions reflecting the triumph of the upper strata. The dominant element within the Party was the so-called 'financial oligarchy' which was composed of a small group of great banking and industrial families headed by the Brătianu family and its close allies.

In the years immediately after the First World War this oligarchy and the leaders of the Liberal Party formed a single entity presided over by Ionel Brătianu, whom the historian Nicolae Iorga called 'the uncrowned king of the country'. The Brătianu group within the Party controlled or influenced the boards of directors of numerous banks and industrial enterprises.

This intertwining of finance, business and politics on a grand scale had been fostered by the state's assumption of a crucial role in promoting economic development beginning in the latter decades of the 19th century.[2] Yet, the predominance of the oligarchy was, paradoxically, undermined by Liberal ideology. To become a genuine and strong national party, Brătianu and his colleagues thought it imperative that they attract other groups. After the War they turned their attention especially to financial and business elites in the newly acquired provinces, in the first instance to the dissident factions of Romanian national parties in Transylvania, Bukovina and Bessarabia. They also welcomed those who could set aside ideology and political animosities and find a place for themselves in a broadly inclusive Liberal Party, notably Conservatives from their now defunct party. While the ranks of the Liberals thus expanded, the newcomers were little constrained by party traditions and had only tenuous links to the oligarchy. Brătianu's management skills were thus put to a severe test in holding the coalition together. He was largely successful; those who came after him were not.

Brătianu's concerns about the unity of the new state were never fully quieted now that the Old Kingdom had joined to itself peoples of ethnic, cultural and religious traditions quite different from those of the Romanians. He could not help suspecting them of harbouring aspirations distinct from his own and those of the majority of Romanians. This, he thought, might tempt irredentist neighbours, notably Hungary and Soviet Russia, to challenge the territorial integrity of Greater Romania.

The multiplicity of political parties was also a source of anxiety. It seemed to him a subtle but by no means negligible threat to national unity. His solution was, in part, legislation. He and his party sponsored the drafting of a new Constitution, which the Chamber of Deputies and the Senate approved and the King promulgated in March 1923. In essence it extended the provisions of the Constitution of 1866 to the new territories. It promised broad civil and political liberties to all citizens, but it left the details of how they would be exercised to the will of future Parliaments; that is, to political parties. It reinforced the centralisation of administration by reaffirming the broad powers of the Ministries in Bucharest and the Prefects in the counties, who were appointed by and responsible to the centre, thereby sharply limiting local authority and initiative. Brătianu also pursued a tightening of what he perceived to be centrifugal forces by promoting a new electoral law in 1926, a measure he hoped would further enhance the power of the Liberals and solidify their role as a national party. The law awarded the party that received at least 40 per cent of the votes a 'premium' in the form of 50 per cent of the seats in the Chamber of Deputies. The winning party also obtained a proportional share of the other half of the seats and thus might end up with over two-thirds of all the seats in the Chamber. Confident of his ability to control the electoral process, Brătianu was thus intent on dominating the legislature in the same way he did the bureaucracy.

Brătianu had to contend with opposition across the political spectrum. The most obstinate and vociferous, and the greatest threat to the Liberal ascendancy, came from the Romanian National Party and the Peasant Party, whose leaders made no secret of their determination to drive the Liberals from power. They were opposed to the new Constitution because they judged it mainly a device intended to make permanent the Liberals' hold on power and they did not hesitate to take their cause to the streets, a tactic that increased Brătianu's doubts about their fitness to govern. In the end, convinced that they could expect success against the Liberals only if they united their two parties, they created the National Peasant Party in 1926, which was headed by Iuliu Maniu and Ion Mihalache, both of whom staunchly supported democratic government. In uniting, they restored the pre-War two-party system that had ceased to function when the Conservative Party disintegrated after the War.[3]

Brătianu had less to fear from the extreme left and the extreme right. The Romanian Communist Party, founded in 1921 by Socialists inspired by the Bolshevik Revolution in Russia, had little appeal for the great majority of Romanians. They (and Brătianu) viewed it as simply an agent of Soviet Russia and continuous scrutiny of the Party by the police culminated in its being outlawed in 1924. On the far right anti-Semitism aroused support from a diversity of classes and groups, but the most important organisation, the League of National Christian Defence, was too undisciplined to pose a serious threat to the Liberals.

Another issue of diversity that Brătianu had to confront was the status of the minorities. The three most significant communities were the Hungarians (roughly 7.9 per cent) and Saxons (roughly 4.1 per cent) of Transylvania and the Jews (4 per cent). Brătianu and Romanian political elites in general, determined as they were to consolidate Greater Romania into a unitary Romanian national state by all the means at their disposal, had no incentive to promote the political aspirations and the cultural and religious autonomy of the minorities. On the other hand, Hungarians, Saxons and Jews, for their part, were equally intent on preserving their ethnic individuality and thus strove to achieve as great a degree of cultural and even political autonomy as possible.

In order to strengthen the national state the Brătianu government reinterpreted or ignored obligations towards the rights of minorities Romania had assumed at the end of the War. Two documents in particular – the Alba Iulia Resolutions of 1918 approved at the time of the union of Transylvania with Romania and the Minorities Treaty drawn up at the Paris Peace Conference in 1919 – set forth the norms that were supposed to govern relations between the government and its minorities. The first accorded the minorities the right to education, public administration and justice in their own languages by persons chosen by them, and the right to be represented in administrative and legislative bodies in accordance with their proportion of the population. As for the Minorities Treaty, the Romanian government promised the international community to protect the rights of its ethnic, language and religious minorities. But, as we have seen, Brătianu strenuously opposed the Treaty; and when Romanian representatives did sign it, they did so with great reluctance, because, as Brătianu put it, the Treaty was simply a means by which outsiders could intervene in Romania's domestic affairs whenever it suited them, thereby jeopardising the integrity of Greater Romania. As a consequence, neither document as such was incorporated into the Romanian Constitution of 1923, nor did Parliament pass legislation making them a part of the new political and legal structures. By declaring

Romania to be a unitary, indivisible national state, the Constitution of 1923 largely ignored the expanded ethnic and cultural diversity brought about by the accession of new territories. Although it indeed assured all citizens equal rights, it offered the minorities individual, not collective, rights – an outcome that fell far short of the aspirations of Hungarians and Germans in Transylvania.

As they modernised the economy and helped bring into being a new society, Brătianu, the oligarchy and their allies were also determined to reserve to Romanians, that is, to themselves, both decision-making and benefits by keeping to a minimum the participation of foreigners in their grand enterprise. Although Brătianu had every intention of maintaining good relations with the industrial and financial powers of Europe, he remained anxious to avoid economic subordination to the West. He and his colleagues were certain that industrialisation was their best means of bringing Romania up to a European level of prosperity and civilisation and of enabling it to be valued as an important regional player by the Great Powers as they pursued their own objectives in Eastern Europe. As well as ensuring that their annual state budgets allocated substantial investment capital to industry and associated branches of the economy, they used the state in other ways to promote their idea of a national economy: laws were passed that required Romanian majorities on boards of directors and a preponderance of Romanian capital in key enterprises; protective tariffs on imports of manufactured goods; and subsidies and tax concessions for protected industries. All these measures contributed to the progress of industry, but no dramatic changes occurred in the proportion of foreign to native capital as the economy still remained dependent on foreign capital.[4]

Despite their commitment to industry as the foundation of Romania's future, the Liberals could not ignore the reality that for the present agriculture was and would be for some time the primary source of national wealth – and, hence, the very sector of the economy from which native investment capital for industry and infrastructure would mainly come. The land reform that Brătianu and his Party had sponsored in the years before the outbreak of the First World War and during the War itself was fulfilled in a series of laws passed by Parliament between 1918 and 1921. Although other parties were in power for most of this period, the Liberals stood behind this legislation. Brătianu and his colleagues were joined by many others of different political persuasions and social classes, even some large landowners, who recognised the futility of maintaining the old agrarian order. Economic conservatives, joining the Liberals, were persuaded that the new organisation of agriculture might well improve efficiency and thus increase productivity and profit. Brătianu and the Liberals, besides considering reform a matter of principle, wanted to make certain that agriculture would serve the needs of the expanding industry and the growing industrial centres by providing abundant raw materials and adequate supplies of inexpensive food. They were also worried by social turmoil in many parts of post-war Europe, especially to the east, in Soviet Russia. Peasant unrest at home, as manifested both in the violence of 1907 (which had remained fresh in the minds of everyone) and more recently in the disaffection evident on the battlefront in Moldavia, convinced them of the need for major social reforms in order to strengthen national solidarity and thereby protect with more certainty the new borders from unforgiving neighbours.

The agrarian reforms of the 1920s, carried out in part

under the auspices of the Liberals, brought about a massive transfer of land from large landowners to smallholders and the landless. Nearly six million hectares were expropriated and distributed to some 1,400,000 peasants. But Brătianu and the Liberals did not thereby solve the agrarian crisis, for, as he himself had acknowledged on numerous occasions, it was not solely an agricultural problem. In the interwar period many forces were at work that continued to keep agriculture and its labour force tied to tradition: a steadily increasing population on the land, the relentless fragmentation of peasant holdings, the uncertainties of the international market, the slow development of industry and, not least, the Liberals' own priorities in economic development. The Liberals' focus on industry, business and banking distracted them from the needs of agriculture and, in a sense, prevented them from formulating and carrying out an aggressive agrarian program. Some modernisation of agriculture was indeed taking place, as the remaining large landholders used machinery and hired hands in place of indentured peasant labour. Yet, within a few years after the expropriation and redistribution of land many peasants found themselves forced again to rent land from landlords and thus fell back into a position of economic dependency, a situation that discouraged innovation and undermined hope.

In foreign policy Brătianu's primary objective was to maintain the international order fashioned at the Paris Peace Conference. The need to protect the frontiers traced in the various peace treaties determined his choice of allies and the main direction of his initiatives. To defend the national interest he was intent on continuing the foreign policy he had adopted in the years just before the outbreak of the First World War: reliance on the Western powers. In this endeavour he had the support of all Romanian political parties, except the Communists who looked to Soviet Russia for guidance. Brătianu and other leading political figures relied on France and, with less certainty, on Britain as the chief guarantors of the Versailles settlement.

Brătianu was not reassured by the course that relations between Romania and its wartime allies took in the immediate post-war era. But he could not have been surprised that ill-feeling and mistrust had survived the signing of peace treaties. First of all, ugly financial matters left over from Versailles intruded into the relationship. The Commission on Reparations, managed by the Great Powers, gave Romanian claims for reparations against the Central Powers little credence and refused even to allow a Romanian delegation to take part in its deliberations. Then, France and Britain pursued an issue raised by Lloyd George at Paris, namely the so-called 'quota of liberation'. He had pointed out that the principal Allies had spent enormous sums to free numerous peoples and thought that the latter should pay at least something in return for their emancipation. The Romanians were given little say in the matter and in 1924 they were assessed 235 million gold francs as their share. Even though Romania was later excused from paying any part of this enormous sum, the whole episode engendered feelings of betrayal in Romanian political circles.

Yet Brătianu and Romanian politicians generally saw no alternative to reliance on France to counter any threat to the Versailles settlement and thus as the protector of Greater Romania from the aggrieved revisionist states – the Soviet Union, Hungary and Bulgaria. But French politicians showed little interest in Romania until the late 1930s, even though Romania formed part of the alliance system in Eastern

Europe patronised by France. An indication of French disinterest was the delay in the signing of a formal alliance until 1926, eight years after the War. Even then, the initiative came from Romania and France avoided a military commitment because its generals doubted the capacity of the Romanian army to wage an effective military campaign and because its politicians rejected any suggestion that France should be obligated to come to Romania's defence in case of war. Nonetheless, Brătianu considered the agreement valuable politically as signifying a unity of interests between the two countries on Eastern Europe, even though in fact French governments thought of the treaty as merely one of many instruments they could use, if they chose, to maintain their influence in the region.[5]

Romania's relations with Great Britain in the interwar period were unremarkable. The absence of closeness, even a feigned one by the Romanians as in the case of France, was due on the one hand to Britain's lack of political interest in Romania and its ill-defined policy toward South-eastern Europe in general and, on the other hand, to the Romanians' own lack of warmth toward a people and culture that had played but a modest part in creating the intellectual climate of modern Romania. British commerce and investments in Romania, all modest except for the oil industry, offered little incentive for closer relations in other fields.[6] As a consequence, Brătianu, like the majority of Romanian politicians, assigned only a secondary role to Britain in his foreign policy calculations.

Despite Brătianu's reliance on the West as the upholders of the Versailles system, he retained his long-standing suspicions about the intentions of the Great Powers toward the smaller states of Europe. He thus sought ways to limit their powers of control and intervention. At first he thought the League of Nations might serve the purpose of giving smaller states a genuine voice in international affairs; but it soon became clear to him that the will of the Great Powers would in all matters prevail. He looked to the Little Entente, created in 1920 and 1921 through bilateral agreements between Romania, Yugoslavia and Czechoslovakia, as a tool for curtailing the Great Powers' habit of deciding matters for the region without consulting the states there. But here, too, his hopes were quickly undone. The Pact of Locarno, concluded in 1925 by the Western powers and Germany, seemed to him business as usual. The signatories agreed on international boundaries in Western Europe, but largely ignored Eastern Europe. He took the occasion to remind himself again that reliance on the Great Powers in international political and economic matters was always a gamble.

In other foreign policy endeavours the results were equally disappointing. Brătianu's efforts to ensure the inviolability of Romania's frontiers to the east and north by negotiation failed. Neither Hungary nor the Soviet Union would recognise the loss of territory to Romania at the end of the War. The dispute over Transylvania prevented any serious rapprochement with Hungary throughout the interwar period, as both countries claimed the territory as an integral part of their respective national states. The same may be said of relations between the Soviet Union and Romania. Here Bessarabia was the bone of contention, as its incorporation into Romania in 1918 had led to a break in relations. Negotiations on and off to find a solution to the dispute resulted in the draft of a non-aggression pact in May 1922; but in November the Soviet Foreign Minister Georgy Chicherin informed Brătianu that if good relations were to prevail between their two countries, Romania would have to evacuate Bessarabia.[7] Substantive talks of any sort during the decade ended in 1924.

After four years as Prime Minister, Brătianu decided by early 1926 that the time had come for a short intermission in direct Liberal Party rule. Unfavourable returns for the Liberals in elections for communal councils and agricultural chambers and growing opposition from other political parties which were certain that their time to govern had come persuaded him to seek another formula for maintaining Liberal influence. He decided that an interim government headed by General Averescu, who became Prime Minister on 30 March 1926, would be the most acceptable solution. But as the head of the largest and most powerful political party in the country, Brătianu, despite earlier experiences with Averescu, had little doubt that his will would prevail and that Averescu would respect the Liberal agenda. Averescu even assured him that he would withdraw as Prime Minister when Brătianu so desired. But in office Averescu once again pursued policies of his own and showed every intention of holding onto power indefinitely. Among the issues that alienated him from Brătianu was the matter of the succession to the throne. Brătianu was utterly opposed to Prince Carol, Ferdinand's older son who in 1925 had renounced his claims to the throne. He had remained in exile in Western Europe, but recently had had a change of heart and was now seeking support from leading politicians for a 'restoration'. Brătianu was repelled by Carol's apparent intention to replace the constitutional monarchy by a more authoritarian royal intervention in political life, a change that would endanger the progress of liberal democracy, not to mention the predominance of the Liberal Party. But Averescu, it seems, supported Carol mainly in the hope that a grateful monarch would retain him as Prime Minister.

Pressure from the Liberals and the King finally proved too much for Averescu to resist, and on 4 June 1927 he resigned. After a short interim government presided over by Brătianu's brother-in-law, Barbu Ştirbey, Brătianu himself returned as Prime Minister on 21 June.

Brătianu's new term of office was too short to enable him to pursue earlier policies with appropriate vigour. A severe blow was the death of King Ferdinand on 19 July 1927.

They had generally agreed on what had to be done to protect Greater Romania and on how to proceed with internal nation building. Although Brătianu had taken the initiative, Ferdinand had provided valuable support through his deep sense of duty and willingness to allow competent politicians the necessary leeway to deal with the country's problems. Brătianu now had the satisfaction of seeing the succession proceed in accordance with agreements reached in 1925: Ferdinand's six-year-old grandson, Mihai, ascended the throne to rule under a regency until he came of age. No public demonstrations in favour of Carol took place.

Many projects remained on Brătianu's agenda, but the usual élan with which he tackled new problems gradually deserted him. He was now 63 and, especially in recent years, the strains of political life had taken their toll on his health. In autumn 1927 he experienced longer periods of fainting, and in November doctors discovered a general deterioration of vital organs which gradually ceased to function. He died on 24 November at his home in Bucharest. His remains were brought to Florica and were laid to rest in the family chapel.

The last photograph taken of Ionel Brătianu, several times Prime Minister of Romania.

III

The Legacy

8

Epilogue

The death of Ionel Brătianu proved to be a turning-point in the history of the Liberal Party and of Romania. None of his successors was as capable of holding together the various factions of the Party and imposing their will on the political life of the country as he had been. His brother Vintilă succeeded him as head of the party and Prime Minister but he proved unable to master the political rivalries within the party and resigned in 1928. The Liberals were out of power until 1933, when Ion G Duca, now head of the Party and the long-time adviser to Ionel Brătianu, was elected. But when he was assassinated by the extreme right Iron Guard sharp divisions within the Liberal Party revealed themselves and it lost cohesion.

The Romania to which Ionel Brătianu had devoted his life and had committed his party had followed the Western European model since the latter decades of the 19th century. In striving to bring the Romanian economy up to a European level, Brătianu and the Liberal Party had promoted industrialisation and the building of a modern infrastructure. Brătianu's successors as custodians of the national economy, in the main, followed the path he had laid out. The Liberals, in power between 1934 and 1937, continued to direct investment mainly to industry and infrastructure and left the structure of agriculture largely unchanged. They did little to improve the living standards of the majority of peasants and continued the long-standing policy of encouraging the production of wheat for the international market as a means of obtaining foreign currency, which they then used to expand industry.

If the economy evolved generally in accordance with the principles Brătianu espoused, political life did not. The 1930s witnessed a steady drift to the right and the replacement by the end of the decade of the Western-style parliamentary system with an authoritarian regime imposed by King Carol II. Partly, this turn of events was the result of the world depression of the early 1930s, which deepened prevailing economic imbalances and sharpened social tensions. The crisis emboldened many in Romania who opposed everything that modern Europe stood for, not only democratic political institutions, but also industry, urbanisation and rationalism which they condemned as foreign to the Romanian 'sense of being'. But partly the crisis of liberal democracy in Romania was caused by the aggressive policies pursued by Nazi Germany and Fascist Italy in the 1930s and the unwillingness of the Western democracies to stand up to their assault on the Versailles system, all of which suggested to both opponents and supporters of democracy in Romania that their country's security would be served best by an accommodation with the authoritarian states.

The liberal Romania that Brătianu had in great measure fashioned suffered a mortal blow on 20 February 1938 when Carol took advantage of the weakness of successive governments to assert his royal authority. He abolished the

Constitution of 1923 and put in its place one that recast the political institutions of the country in a new mould based on corporatist principles and granting the King full powers to rule. Carol dissolved all political parties and groupings, imposed harsh penalties on anyone who opposed his authority and ordered the assassination of Corneliu Zelea Codreanu, leader of the Iron Guard, which he had come to regard as a dangerous rival.[1]

The foreign policy that Ionel Brătianu had promoted was also steadily undermined in the 1930s. It had relied on France and Britain as the chief guarantors of the international order devised at Paris. But as Nazi Germany gained the initiative in European affairs King Carol strove to accommodate Romania to Adolf Hitler's new order.

It was the outbreak of war and decisive events on the Western Front that finally brought the dramatic shift in Romania's foreign policy. German victories in the Low Countries and northern France in May 1940 convinced Carol and his advisers that the Allied cause was lost and that Romania had no choice but to seek a place in German-dominated Europe. The new direction was made manifest in the so-called 'Oil Treaty' that Romania signed with Germany on 29 May, in which Romania promised to deliver a fixed quantity of oil at 1939 prices in return for military equipment.

As the First World War had made possible the achievement of Ionel Brătianu's Greater Romania by shaking prevailing Imperial structures, so now the Second World War led to the dissolution of his (and every patriotic Romanian's) sense of national destiny fulfilled. Greater Romania quickly unravelled as the revisionist powers hastened to present their bills once the architects of Versailles – France, which had been defeated on the battlefield, and Britain, which had shared in that defeat and had been driven from the continent – were no longer able to offer Romania even token cover. In the summer of 1940 the Soviet Union demanded the 'return' of Bessarabia and the cession of northern Bukovina and got both; Bulgaria recovered southern Dobrudja; and Hungary obtained north Transylvania through Hitler's 'arbitration' at Vienna in August. The Vienna Diktat, as the agreement came to be called, marked the end of an independent Romanian foreign policy and the subordination of the Romanian economy to the German war effort.

King Carol could not survive. He was forced to abdicate on 6 September 1940, an event that was followed by the proclamation of an authoritarian National Legionary State headed by General Ion Antonescu. In January 1941 he established a full-fledged military dictatorship, which was to remain in place until August 1944 and which attached Romania still more tightly to the German war effort including the ill-fated assault on the Soviet Union.

The catastrophe (in the eyes of the majority of Romanians) that overtook the remnants of Brătianu's Romania – the Soviet occupation – could not be averted. As the Red Army stood once again at the Prut River ready to invade Romania with overwhelming numbers, King Mihai, who had succeeded his father, and a coalition of political leaders had General Antonescu arrested. On the same day, 23 August 1944, the King announced that the country had joined the Allied cause against Germany.

The Romania that had been evolving since the first half of the 19th century within the traditions and spirit of Western and Central European nation-building was now replaced by another Romania. In the three years following the overthrow of the Antonescu dictatorship the country was relentlessly drawn to the East. Occupation by the Soviet army and the rapid rise to power by the Romanian Communist Party under the patronage of the Soviet Communist Party led to the undermining of existing political and social structures and their replacement of its intellectual and spiritual foundations by an alien ethos. The abdication of King Mihai on 30 December 1947 and the proclamation of the Romanian People's Republic immediately after signified the incorporation of Romania within the Soviet sphere. Parliamentary government, the multi-party system, the capitalist, entrepreneurial spirit in the economy, the unrestrained debate about identity and almost everything else characteristic of the Romania that Ionel Brătianu had striven to put in place were swept away.

Notes

Introduction

1. His full name was Ion I C Brătianu, but he was usually called Ionel Brătianu in order to distinguish him from his father, Ion C Brătianu. It is the practice I follow in this book.
2. This was the official designation. I shall use simply 'Liberal Party', as was commonly done at the time.

1: Beginnings, 1864–1895

1. Ioan C Filitti, *Principatele Române de la 1828 la 1834* (Bucureşti, 1934) pp 238–370.
2. Apostol Stan, *Ion C. Brătianu. Un promotor al liberalismului în România* (Bucureşti, 1993) pp 28–30, 33.
3. L Boicu, Gh Platon and Al Zub (eds), *Cuza Voda in memoriam* (Iaşi, 1973) pp 503–50.
4. *Din corespondenţa familiei I. C. Brătianu, 1859–1881*, Vol 1 (Bucureşti, 1933), pp 265–6; hereafter *Corespondenţa*.
5. *Corespondenţa*, Vol 3 (Bucureşti, 1934), pp 382–3.
6. *Corespondenţa*, Vol 3, p 226.

7. *Corespondența*, Vol 2 (București, 1934) pp 277–81.
8. *Corespondența*, Vol 2, p 286.
9. For a succinct appraisal, see Bogdan Murgescu, *România și Europa* (Iași, 2010) pp 130–48.

2: Apprenticeship and Reform, 1895–1914

1. Nicolae Bănescu, *Ion I. C. Brătianu (1864–1927)* (Craiova, 1931) p 17.
2. Matei Dogan, *Analiza statistică a "democrației parlamentare" din România* (București, 1946) pp 10–14.
3. *Discursurile lui Ion I. C. Brătianu*, George Fotino (ed), Vol 1 (București, 1933), pp 10–11, hereafter Brătianu, *Discursurile*.
4. Marie, Queen of Roumania, *The Story of My Life* (New York, 1934) Vol 1, pp. 422–3.
5. Brătianu, *Discursurile*, Vol 2 (București, 1933) p 115.
6. Z Ornea, *Sămănătorismul*, 2nd ed (București, 1971) pp 131–77.
7. Z Ornea, *Poporanismul* (București, 1972) pp 174–97, 242–53.
8. P S Aurelian, *Opere economice*, Mihai C Demetrescu, ed, (București, 1967) pp lx–lxiii, lxviii–lxxiii.
9. Sterie Diamandi, *Galeria oamenilor politici* (București, 1991) p 39.
10. Brătianu, *Discursurile*, Vol 2, pp 477–9.
11. Brătianu, *Discursurile*, Vol 2, p 462.
12. Brătianu, *Discursurile*, Vol 1, pp 345–7; Vol 2, p 20.
13. Brătianu, *Discursurile*, Vol 1, p 430.
14. Brătianu, *Discursurile*, Vol 4 (București, 1940) pp 21–3.
15. Brătianu, *Discursurile*, Vol 4, p 17.
16. Apostol Stan and Mircea Iosa, *Liberalismul politic în România* (București, 1996) p 354.

17. Anastasie Iordache, *Ion I. C. Brătianu* (Bucureşti: 1994) pp 168–9, 175.

18. Iordache, *Brătianu*, pp 176–7.

19. Brătianu, *Discursurile*, Vol 4, pp 160–3.

20. Brătianu, *Discursurile*, Vol 4, p 161.

3: Great Powers, Small Powers, 1909–1914

1. Gheorghe Nicolae Căzan and Şerban Rădulescu-Zoner, *România şi Tripla Alianţă* (Bucureşti, 1979) p 281.

2. *Die Grosse Politik der Europäischen Kabinette, 1871–1914* Vol 27 (Berlin, 1925), pp 197–8, 201–06.

3. Claudiu-Lucian Topor, *Germania, România şi războaiele balcanice* (Iaşi, 2008) pp 49–50.

4. Topor, *Germania, România*, p 100.

5. Brătianu, *Discursurile*, Vol 4, p 33.

6. Brătianu, *Discursurile*, Vol 4, pp 19–21.

7. Vintilă Brătianu, *Scrieri şi cuvântări* (Bucureşti, 1940) Vol 3, pp 274–5.

8. Iuliu Maniu, *Discursuri parlamentare (29 maiu-31 iulie 1906)* (Blaj, 1906) pp 76–7.

9. Teodor Pavel, *Mişcarea Românilor pentru unitatea naţională şi diplomaţia puterilor centrale* (Timişoara, 1982) Vol 2 (1894–1914), p 116.

10. Kommission für Neuere Geschichte Österreichs, *Österreich-Ungarns Aussenpolitik von der Bosnischen Krise 1908 bis zum Kriegsausbruch 1914. Diplomatische Aktenstücke des Osterreichisch-Ungarischen Ministeriums des Äussern* (Vienna, 1930) Vol 7, pp 611–2, 628.

11. Topor, *Germania, România*, p 197.

4: Neutrality, 1914–1916

1. *Documents diplomatiques concernant les rapports entre l'Autriche-Hongrie et la Roumanie (22 juillet-27 août 1916)* (Vienna, 1916) p 3.
2. Iordache, *Brătianu*, pp 218–21.
3. *1918 la Români* (Bucureşti, 1983) Vol 1, p 453.
4. Glenn E Torrey, *Romania and World War I* (Iaşi, 1998) p 17.
5. *1918 la Români*, Vol 1, p 508.
6. *1918 la Români*, Vol 1, pp 521–2.
7. Constantin Nuţu, *România în anii neutralităţii, 1914–1916* (Bucureşti, 1972) pp 239–40, 250.
8. *1918 la Români*, Vol 1, pp 522–4, 537–8, 576–8.
9. Nuţu, *România*, p 299.
10. Glenn E Torrey, 'Rumania's Decision to Intervene: Brătianu and the Entente, June-July 1916', *Rumanian Studies*, Vol 2 (1973), pp 3–29.
11. C J Lowe, 'The Failure of British Diplomacy in the Balkans, 1914–1916', *Canadian Journal of History*, Vol 4, No 1 (1969), pp 73–97.
12. V I Vinogradov, *Rumyniia v gody pervoi mirovoi voiny* (Moscow, 1969) pp 158–9.

5: War, 1916–1918

1. Ion G Duca, *Amintiri politice* Vol 1 (Munich, 1981), p 276.
2. Duca, *Amintiri*, Vol 1, p 277.
3. Alexandru Marghiloman, *Note politice (1897–1924)* (Bucureşti, 1927) Vol 2 (1916–1917), p 151.
4. Duca, *Amintiri*, Vol 1, p 284.
5. Duca, *Amintiri*, Vol 1, p 284.
6. Glenn E Torrey, *Henri Mathias Berthelot. Soldier of*

France, Defender of Romania (Iaşi, 2001) pp 141–227.

7. Adolf Köster, *Die Sturmschar Falkenhayns. Kriegsberichte aus Siebenbürgen und Rumänien* (Munich, 1917) pp 93–118.

8. Brătianu, *Discursurile*, Vol 4, p 417.

9. Iordache, *Brătianu*, pp 335–40.

10. Duca, *Amintiri*, Vol 2 (Munich, 1981), pp 170–1, 184–5.

11. Keith Hitchins, 'The Russian Revolution and the Rumanian Socialist Movement, 1917–1918', *Slavic Review*, Vol 27, No 2 (1968), pp 270–3.

12. Alberto Basciani, *La difficile unione. La Bessarabia e la Grande Romania, 1918–1940*, 2nd ed (Rome, 2007), pp 72–96.

13. Ioan Scurtu, *Ion I. C. Brătianu* (Bucureşti, 1992) pp 44–5.

14. Duca, *Amintiri*, Vol 3 (Munich, 1982), p 71.

15. Duca, *Amintiri*, Vol 3, pp 15–16, 55–6.

16. P Cazacu, *Moldova dintre Prut şi Nistru, 1812–1918* (Iaşi, n. d.) pp 315–21.

6: Peace, 1919

1. Gheorghe I Brătianu, *Acţiunea politică şi militară a României în 1919*, 2nd ed (Bucureşti, 1940) pp 44–6.

2. Brătianu, *Acţiunea*, pp 59–60.

3. Lucian Leuştean, *România, Ungaria şi Tratatul de la Trianon, 1918–1920* (Iaşi, 2002) pp 180–1.

4. *Foreign Relations of the United States, The Paris Peace Conference, 1919*, Vol 2 (Washington, D.C., 1942), pp 265–6; hereafter *FRUS*.

5. Maria, Regina României, *Însemnări zilnice (decembrie 1918-decembrie 1919)* (Bucureşti, 1996) Vol 1, p 78.

6. Iordache, *Brătianu*, p 436, citing the Library of the

Romanian Academy, Bucharest, Arhiva Ion I. C. Brătianu, Mapa 2, Varia 7.

7. *FRUS*, Vol 3 (Washington, D. C., 1943) pp 830–4.

8. Leuştean, *România*, pp. 53–6.

9. Ion Stanciu, 'Un nou document privitor la acţiunea politică şi militară a României în aprilie 1919', *Revista Istorică*, new series, Vol 1, No 1 (1990), pp 187–91.

10. Brătianu, *Acţiunea*, pp 62–4.

11. *FRUS*, Vol 3, pp 396–7.

12. Sherman David Spector, *Romania at the Paris Peace Conference* (Iaşi, 1995) pp 253–65.

13. *România în anii Primului Război Mondial* Vol 2 (Bucureşti, 1987) pp 695–700.

7: Greater Romania, 1919–1927

1. Mihail Rusenescu and Ioan Scurtu, *Viaţa politică în România, 1922–1928* (Bucureşti, 1979) pp 40–7.

2. Constantin Nica, *Liberalismul din România – teorie şi practică* (Bucureşti, 2007) Vol 3, pp 201–10, 278–321.

3. I Ciupercă, *Opoziţie şi putere în România anilor 1922– 1928* (Iaşi, 1994) pp 174–209.

4. Murgescu, *România şi Europa* (Iaşi, 2010) pp 250–67.

5. Constantin Iordan-Sima, 'Despre negocierele privind încheierea alianţei franco-române (10 iunie 1926)', *Revista de Istorie*, Vol 29, No 2 (1976), pp 223–31.

6. Valeriu Florin Dobrinescu, *Relaţii româno-engleze (1914–1933)* (Iaşi, 1986) pp 83–148.

7. Emilian Bold and Răzvan Ovidiu Locovei, *Relaţii româno-sovietice (1918–1941)* (Iaşi, 2008) pp 75–104.

8: Epilogue

1. Ioan Scurtu, *Carol al II-lea* (Bucureşti, 2001) pp 218–39.

Chronology

YEAR	AGE	THE LIFE AND THE LAND
1864	0	Born at family estate: Florica, Argeş County.
		Agrarian Reform Law.
1866	2	Prince Alexandru Cuza forced to abdicate; succeeded by Karl of Hohenzollern-Sigmaringen
		Constitution promulgated; remains in force with some amendments until 1923.
		Electoral law enacted based on limited franchise reserving power to upper classes.
1869	5	Romanian National Party created in Transylvania.

YEAR	HISTORY	CULTURE
1864	Schleswig War: Austrian and Prussian troops defeat Danes.	Charles Dickens, *Our Mutual Friend*.
	Archduke Maximilian of Austria crowned Emperor of Mexico.	Leo Tolstoy, *War and Peace* (-1869).
	US Civil War: General Ulysses S Grant made Commander-in-Chief of Union Army, General William Sherman marches through Georgia.	
	Abraham Lincoln re-elected US President.	
1866	Austro-Prussian War: Prussian victory at Sadowa, end of German Confederation.	Fyodor Dostoevsky, *Crime and Punishment*.
	Venice votes to join Italy.	
	Revolts in Crete against Turkish rule.	
	Robert Whitehead invents locomotive torpedo.	
1869	Greece agrees to leave Crete.	R D Blackmore, *Lorna Doone*.
	Red River Rebellion begins in Canada.	Mark Twain, *The Innocents Abroad*.
	Opening of Suez Canal.	Richard Wagner, *Rheingold*.

YEAR	AGE	THE LIFE AND THE LAND
1875	11	Liberal groups lay foundation of National Liberal Party.
1876	12	Liberal government formed under Ion C Brătianu, who remains Prime Minister except for a few months until 1888.
1877	13	Romania and Russia sign convention allowing Russian troops to cross Romania to attack Ottoman Empire.
		Romanian Parliament votes for war against Ottoman Empire.
		Romanian Parliament declares Romania independent state.
1878	14	Armistice agreed to by Russia, Romania and Ottoman Empire, ending Romania's War for Independence.
		Congress of Berlin: Great Powers award Romania Dobrudja in exchange for southern Bessarabia, ceded to Russia.
		Ionel Brătianu's family moves to Bucharest.

YEAR	HISTORY	CULTURE
1875	Risings in Bosnia and Herzegovina against Turkish rule.	Mark Twain, *The Adventures of Tom Sawyer*.
	Prince of Wales visits India.	W S Gilbert and Arthur Sullivan, *Trial by Jury*.
	Britain buys Suez Canal shares from Khedive of Egypt.	
	Captain Matthew Webb first man to swim English Channel.	
1876	Turkish troops massacre Bulgarians.	Henry James, *Roderick Hudson*.
	Ottoman Sultan deposed.	Auguste Renoir, *Le Moulin de la Galette*.
	Serbia and Montenegro declare war on Ottoman Empire.	First complete performance of Richard Wagner's *Ring Cycle* at Bayreuth.
	New Ottoman constitution proclaimed.	
	Alexander Graham Bell invents telephone.	
	Rutherford B Hayes elected US President.	
1877	Queen Victoria proclaimed Empress of India.	Henry James, *The American*.
	Russo-Turkish War begins.	Auguste Rodin, *The Age of Bronze*.
	Satsuma rebellion suppressed in Japan.	
	Thomas A Edison invents the phonograph.	
1878	Russo-Turkish War: Ottoman Empire seeks armistice, British fleet arrives off Constantinople, armistice signed.	Thomas Hardy, *The Return of the Native*.
	Congress of Berlin discusses Eastern Question.	Algernon Charles Swinburne, *Poems and Ballads*.
	Electric street lighting introduced in London.	Ruskin-Whistler libel case.

YEAR	AGE	THE LIFE AND THE LAND
1880	16	Great Britain, France and Germany formally recognise Romania's independence.
		Conservative groups merge to establish Conservative Party.
1881	17	Parliament proclaims Romania kingdom; Carol I crowned King.
		National School of Bridges and Roads founded in Bucharest.
1882	18	Graduates from St Sava National College, Bucharest.
1883	19	Enters Lycée Sainte-Barbe in Paris to prepare for engineering studies.
		Romania signs secret treaty of alliance with Austria-Hungary and Germany; foundation of Romania's foreign policy until eve of First World War.

YEAR	HISTORY	CULTURE
1880	France annexes Tahiti.	George Eliot dies.
	Transvaal Republic declares independence from Britain.	Fyodor Dostoevsky, *The Brothers Karamazov*.
	Pacific War: Chile vs Bolivia and Peru (-1884).	Auguste Rodin, *The Thinker*.
	James Garfield elected US President.	
1881	First Boer War: British defeated at Majuba Hill, Treaty of Pretoria recognises independence of Transvaal.	Henry James, *Portrait of a Lady*.
		Jacques Offenbach, *Les Contes d'Hoffmann*.
	US President James Garfield assassinated; Chester A Arthur succeeds him.	Natural History Museum opens in London.
	Austro-Serbian treaty of alliance signed.	
	Pogroms against Jews in Russia.	
1882	Triple Alliance between Italy, Germany and Austria-Hungary.	Robert Louis Stevenson, *Treasure Island*.
	British occupy Cairo.	Leslie Stephen, *Science of Ethics*.
	Hiram Maxim patents his machine gun.	Richard Wagner, *Parsifal*.
		Peter Tchaikovsky, *1812 Overture*.
1883	French gain control of Tunis.	Richard Wagner dies.
	British decide to evacuate the Sudan.	Friedrich Nietzsche, *Thus Spake Zarathustra*.
	Orient Express (Paris-Constantinople) makes first run.	

YEAR	AGE	THE LIFE AND THE LAND
1884	20	Brătianu begins engineering studies at Polytechnic School, Paris.
1886	22	Visits England; much impressed by London.
		Continues engineering studies at School of Bridges and Highways.
1888	24	Ion C Brătianu forced to resign as Prime Minister, retires from political life.
		Travels to northern France and Belgium to observe engineering projects.
1889	25	Prince Ferdinand of Hohenzollern-Sigmaringen, nephew of Carol I, becomes heir to Romanian throne.
		Takes final exams, receives engineering degree; returns home, begins working under Anghel Saligny on expansion of national railroad network.

YEAR	HISTORY	CULTURE
1884	General Gordon arrives in Khartoum.	Mark Twain, *Huckleberry Finn.*
	Germans occupy South-West Africa.	*Oxford English Dictionary* begins publication (-1928).
	Berlin Conference of 14 nations on African affairs.	Georges-Pierre Seurat, *Une Baignade à Asnières.*
	Gold discovered in the Transvaal.	
	Grover Cleveland elected US President.	
1886	British Prime Minister William Gladstone introduces Irish Home Rule Bill.	Robert Louis Stevenson, *Dr Jekyll and Mr Hyde.*
	First Indian National Congress meets.	Frances Hodgson Burnett, *Little Lord Fauntleroy.*
	Canadian-Pacific Railway completed.	Karl Marx's *Das Kapital* published in English.
		Auguste Rodin, *The Kiss.*
1888	Kaiser Wilhelm II accedes to German throne.	Rudyard Kipling, *Plain Tales from the Hills.*
	Suez Canal Convention.	Peter Tchaikovsky, *Symphony No 5.*
	'Jack the Ripper' murders in London.	Vincent Van Gogh, *The Yellow Chair.*
	Benjamin Harrison, grandson of ninth President, elected US President.	
1889	Austro-Hungarian Crown Prince Rudolf commits suicide at Mayerling.	Jerome K Jerome, *Three Men in a Boat.*
	London Dock Strike..	Richard Strauss, *Don Juan.*

YEAR	AGE	THE LIFE AND THE LAND
1891	27	Abandons engineering for politics.
1893	29	Founding congress of Social Democratic Party of Workers of Romania.
1895	31	Wins first election, seat in parliament as Liberal candidate from Gorj County.

YEAR	HISTORY	CULTURE
1891	Triple Alliance (Austria-Hungary, Germany, Italy) renewed for 12 years. German Kaiser Wilhelm II visits London. Franco-Russian entente. Young Turk Movement founded in Vienna.	Thomas Hardy, *Tess of the D'Urbervilles*. Gustav Mahler, *Symphony No 1*. Henri de Toulouse-Lautrec produces first music-hall posters.
1893	Franco-Russian alliance signed. British House of Lords rejects second Irish Home Rule Bill. France acquires protectorate over Laos. Benz constructs his four-wheel car.	Oscar Wilde, *A Woman of No Importance*. Art Nouveau appears in Europe. Giacomo Puccini, *Manon Lescaut*.
1895	Sino-Japanese War ends. Armenians massacred in Ottoman Empire. Jameson Raid into Transvaal. Cuba rebels against Spanish rule. Guglielmo Marconi invents radio telegraphy.	H G Wells, *The Time Machine*. W B Yeats, *Poems*. Peter Tchaikovsky, *Swan Lake*.

YEAR	AGE	THE LIFE AND THE LAND
1897–9	33–35	Minister of Public Works in Liberal government.
1898	34	Birth out of wedlock of only child, Gheorghe I Brătianu.
		Marries Princess Maria Moruzi, mother of Gheorghe; marriage soon ends in divorce.
1899	35	Welcomes former leaders of Social Democratic Party (*generoşi*) into Liberal Party.

YEAR	HISTORY	CULTURE
1897	Klondike (Yukon, Alaska) Gold Rush begins.	H G Wells, *The Invisible Man.*
	Britain's Queen Victoria celebrates Diamond Jubilee.	Edmond Rostand, *Cyrano de Bergerac.*
	Crete proclaims union with Greece: Ottoman Empire declares war, defeated in Thessaly; Peace of Constantinople.	
	Russia occupies Port Arthur.	
	Zionist Congress in Basel, Switzerland.	
1898	Dreyfus case: Émile Zola publishes *J'Accuse* letter.	Thomas Hardy, *Wessex Poems.*
	Horatio H Kitchener defeats Mahdists at Omdurman.	Henry James, *The Turn of the Screw.*
	Spanish-American War: US gain Cuba, Puerto Rico, Guam and the Philippines.	Oscar Wilde, *The Ballad of Reading Gaol.*
	Paris Métro opens.	
	Germany's Otto von Bismarck dies.	
1899	Anglo-Egyptian Sudan Convention.	Rudyard Kipling, *Stalky and Co.*
	Second Boer War begins: British defeats at Stormberg, Magersfontein and Colenso ('Black Week').	Arthur Pinero, *Trelawny of the Wells.*
	First Peace Conference at the Hague.	Edward Elgar, *Enigma Variations.*
	Alfred Dreyfus pardoned by presidential decree.	
	Germany secures Baghdad railway contract.	

YEAR	AGE	THE LIFE AND THE LAND
1901– 02	37–38	Minister of Public Works.

YEAR	HISTORY	CULTURE
1901– 02	Britain's Queen Victoria dies: Edward VII becomes King.	First five Nobel Prizes awarded.
	US President William McKinley assassinated: Theodore Roosevelt succeeds him.	Thomas Mann, *Die Buddenbrooks*.
		August Strindberg, *Dance of Death*.
	Negotiations for Anglo-German alliance end without agreement.	Rudyard Kipling, *Kim*.
	First transatlantic radio signal transmitted.	Pablo Picasso's 'Blue Period' begins.
	Anglo-Japanese Treaty recognises independence of China and Korea.	Arthur Conan Doyle, *The Hound of the Baskervilles*.
		Maxim Gorki, *Lower Depths*.
	Treaty of Vereeniging ends Boer War.	Anton Chekhov, *Three Sisters*.
		Claude Monet, *Waterloo Bridge*.
	First meeting of Committee of Imperial Defence.	Edward Elgar, *Pomp and Circumstance March No 1*.
	Triple Alliance between Austria, Germany and Italy renewed for another six years.	
	USA acquires perpetual control over Panama Canal.	

YEAR	AGE	THE LIFE AND THE LAND
1902– 04	38– 40	Minister of Foreign Affairs.
1906	42	Peasant Party (Partidul Ţărănesc) formed.

YEAR	HISTORY	CULTURE
1903–04	King Alexander I of Serbia murdered. Beginning of Entente Cordiale: King Edward VII of Britain visits Paris, French President Loubet visits London. Russian Social Democratic Party splits into Mensheviks and Bolsheviks (led by Lenin and Trotsky) at its London Congress. Wright Brothers' first flight. Entente Cordiale settles British-French colonial differences. Russo-Japanese War begins. Theodore Roosevelt elected US President. Photoelectric cell invented.	Henry James, *The Ambassadors.* George Bernard Shaw, *Man and Superman.* Jack London, *The Call of the Wild.* Anton Bruckner, *Symphony No. 9.* Film: *The Great Train Robbery.* J M Barrie, *Peter Pan.* Giacomo Puccini, *Madame Butterfly.* Thomas Hardy, *The Dynasts.* Anton Chekhov, *The Cherry Orchard.* Henri Rousseau, *The Wedding.* Sigmund Freud, *The Psychopathology of Everyday Life.*
1906	Edward VII of England and Kaiser Wilhelm II of Germany meet. Britain grants self-government to Transvaal and Orange River Colonies. British ultimatum forces Turkey to cede Sinai Peninsula to Egypt. Armand Fallieres elected President of France. Joao Franco becomes Prime Minister of Spain. Alfred Dreyfus rehabilitated in France. Major earthquake in San Francisco USA kills over 1,000.	John Galsworthy, *A Man of Property.* O Henry, *The Four Million.* Edward Dent founds *Everyman's Library.* Andre Derain, *Port of London.* Jules Massenet, *Ariane.* First jukebox invented.

YEAR	AGE	THE LIFE AND THE LAND
1907	43	Appointed Minister of Interior: responsible for suppressing great peasant uprising which began on 21 Feb. Marries Elisa Știrbey, grand-daughter of Prince Barbu Știrbey, ruler of Wallachia (1849–53).
1908	44	Democratic-Conservative Party formed by Take Ionescu.

YEAR	HISTORY	CULTURE
1907	British and French agree on Siamese independence.	Joseph Conrad, *The Secret Agent*.
	New Zealand granted Dominion status.	Maxim Gorky, *Mother*.
		R M Rilke, *Neue Gedichte*.
	Britain's Edward VII in Rome, Paris and Marienbad, where he meets Russian Foreign Minister Izvolski.	First Cubist exhibition in Paris.
		Pablo Picasso, *Les Demoiselles D'Avignon*.
	Grigori Rasputin gains influence at court of Tsar Nicholas II.	Edvard Munch, *Amor and Psyche*.
	Peace Conference held in The Hague.	Frederick Delius, *A Village Romeo and Juliet*.
1908	*The Daily Telegraph* publishes German Kaiser Wilhelm II's hostile remarks towards England.	Colette, *La Retraite Sentimentale*.
		E M Forster, *A Room with a View*.
	Union of South Africa established.	Kenneth Grahame, *The Wind in the Willows*.
	King Carlos I of Portugal and Crown Prince assassinated: Manuel II becomes King.	Anatole France, *Penguin Island*.
		Marc Chagall, *Nu Rouge*.
	Britain's Edward VII and Russia's Tsar Nicholas II meet at Reval.	Maurice de Vlaminck, *The Red Trees*.
	Ferdinand I declares Bulgaria's independence, assumes title of Tsar.	Bela Bartok, *String Quartet NO.1*.
	William Howard Taft elected US President.	Edward Elgar, *Symphony No. 1 in A-Flat*.

YEAR	AGE	THE LIFE AND THE LAND
1909	45	Becomes Prime Minister: tenure will last until 11 Jan 1911.
		Congress of Liberal Party elects him president of party, position he holds until death in 1927.
1911	47	Promotes 'Liberal Manifesto' setting forth strategy for economic and political reform, goals he pursues to outbreak of war in 1914.
1912	48	First Balkan War: urges mobilisation and intervention as best way to protect Romania's interests.

YEAR	HISTORY	CULTURE
1909	Britain's Edward VII makes state visits to Berlin and Rome. Anglo-German discussions on control of Baghdad railway. Turkish nationalists force Kiamil Pasha, Grand Vizier of Turkey, to resign. Plastic (Bakelite) invented.	H G Wells, *Tono-Bungay*. Marinetti publishes *First Futurist Manifesto*. Richard Strauss, *Elektra*. Frederick Delius, *A Mass of Life*. Henri Matisse, *The Dance*. Vasily Kandinksy paints first abstract paintings.
1911	US-Japanese and Anglo-Japanese commercial treaties signed. German gunboat *Panther* arrives in Agadir: triggers international crisis. Russian Premier Peter Stolypyn assassinated. Italy declares war on Turkey.	Cubism becomes public phenomenon in Paris. Max Beerbohm, *Zuleika Dobson*. D H Lawrence, *The White Peacock*. Saki (H H Munro), *The Chronicles of Clovis*. George Bracque, *Man with a Guitar*. Richard Strauss, *Der Rosenkavalier*. Igor Stravinsky, *Petrushka*.
1912	*Titanic* sinks: 1,513 die. First Balkan War begins: Montenegro declares war on Turkey, Turkey declares war on Bulgaria and Serbia, Turkey asks Great Powers to intervene to end war. Woodrow Wilson elected US President. Lenin establishes connection with Stalin, takes over *Pravda* editorship.	C G Jung, *The Theory of Psychoanalysis*. Marc Chagall, *The Cattle Dealer*. Marcel Duchamp, *Nude descending a staircase II*. Arnold Schoenberg, *Pierrot Lunaire*. Maurice Ravel, *Daphne et Chloe*.

YEAR	AGE	THE LIFE AND THE LAND
1913	49	Second Balkan War: takes part in campaign against Bulgaria.
1914	50	Becomes Prime Minister.
		Engages in polemics with Luigi Luzzatti over situation of Jews in Romania.
		Presses forward with agrarian and electoral reforms, but outbreak of War causes postponement of any action.
		Crown Council approves his proposal for declaration of Romania's neutrality.
		King Carol I dies, succeeded by Ferdinand.

YEAR	HISTORY	CULTURE
1913	London Ambassadors Conference ends 1st Balkan War: establishes independent Albania. King George I of Greece assassinated: succeeded by Constantine I. Second Balkan War begins and ends. US Federal Reserve System established. Mahatma Gandhi, leader of Indian Passive Resistance Movement, arrested.	D H Lawrence, *Sons and Lovers.* Thomas Mann, *Death in Venice.* Marcel Proust, *Du côté de chez Swann.* Igor Stravinsky, *Le Sacre du Printemps.* 'Armory Show' introduces cubism and post-impressionism to New York. Grand Central Station in New York completed.
1914	Archduke Franz Ferdinand of Austria-Hungary and wife assassinated in Sarajevo. First World War begins: Battles of Mons, the Marne and First Ypres; trench warfare on Western Front; Russians defeated in Battles of Tannenberg and Masurian Lakes.	James Joyce, *Dubliners.* Theodore Dreiser, *The Titan.* Gustav Holst, *The Planets.* Matisse, *The Red Studio.* Georges Braque, *Music.* Film: Charlie Chaplin in *Making a Living.*

YEAR	AGE	THE LIFE AND THE LAND
1916	52	Signs military and political conventions with Entente setting forth conditions for Romania's entrance into War.
		Crown Council approves his proposal that Romania join Entente in War against Central Powers; Romania declares war on Austria-Hungary.
		German troops enter Bucharest.
1917	53	Meets with Allied officials in Petrograd; discuss military operations, provisioning on Moldavian front.
		Makes second trip to Petrograd; meets Kerensky, other leaders of new government after March Revolution.
		6 May: Introduces new agrarian, electoral reform laws in parliament.
		Battles of Mărăşti, Mărăşeşti, Oituz.
		Romania signs armistice with Central Powers at Focşani.

YEAR	HISTORY	CULTURE
1916	First World War: Battles of Verdun, the Somme and Jutland.	Lionel Curtis, *The Commonwealth of Nations.*
	US President Woodrow Wilson re-elected.	James Joyce, *Portrait of an Artist as a Young Man.*
	Wilson issues Peace Note to belligerents in European war.	Vicente Blasco Ibanez, *The Four Horsemen of the Apocalypse.*
	David Lloyd George becomes British Prime Minister.	Henri Matisse, *The Three Sisters.*
	Development and use of first effective tanks.	Claude Monet, *Waterlilies.*
		'Dada' movement produces iconoclastic 'anti-art'.
		Richard Strauss, *Ariadne auf Naxos.*
		Film: *Intolerance.*
1917	First World War: Battle of Passchendaele (Third Ypres); British and Commonwealth forces take Jerusalem; USA declares war on Germany; China declares war on Germany and Russia.	P G Wodehouse, *The Man With Two Left Feet.*
		T S Eliot, *Prufrock and Other Observations.*
		Leon Feuchtwanger, *Jud Suess.*
	February Revolution in Russia.	Piet Mondrian launches *De Stijl* magazine in Holland.
	Balfour Declaration favouring establishment of national home for Jewish People in Palestine.	Pablo Picasso designs 'surrealist' costumes, set for Erik Satie's *Parade.*
	German and Russian delegates sign armistice at Brest-Litovsk.	Sergei Prokofiev, *Classical Symphony.*
		Film: *Easy Street.*

YEAR	AGE	THE LIFE AND THE LAND
1918	54	Brătianu resigns as Prime Minister.
		Moldavian Democratic Republic in Bessarabia declares for union with Romania.
		Romania leaves the War under terms of Treaty of Bucharest with Central Powers.
		King Ferdinand orders army to resume hostilities against Central Powers.
		Ferdinand returns to Bucharest.
		Romanians of Transylvania proclaim union of Transylvania, Banat and parts of eastern Hungary with Romania.
		Brătianu becomes Prime Minister in new Liberal government.
1919	55	Brătianu arrives in Paris for the Peace Conference; presents Romania's case before Supreme Council; Supreme Council rebukes Brătianu for refusal to accept proposals for demarcation line between Romanian and Hungarian forces; leaves Paris, returns to Bucharest.
		Romanian troops occupy Budapest.
		Resigns as Prime Minister.
		Romania signs Treaty of Neuilly, defining boundaries with Bulgaria; signs Austrian and Minorities Treaties.

YEAR	HISTORY	CULTURE
1918	First World War: Peace Treaty of Brest-Litovsk signed between Russia and Central Powers; German Spring offensives on Western Front fail; Romania signs Peace of Bucharest with Germany and Austria-Hungary; Allied offensives on Western Front have German army in full retreat; Armistice signed between Allies and Germany; German Fleet surrenders. Ex-Tsar Nicholas II and family executed. Kaiser Wilhelm II of Germany abdicates.	Alexander Blok, *The Twelve*. Gerald Manley Hopkins, *Poems*. Luigi Pirandello, *Six Characters in Search of an Author*. Bela Bartok, *Bluebeard's Castle*. Giacomo Puccini, *Il Trittico*. Gustav Cassel, *Theory of Social Economy*. Oskar Kokoschka, *Friends* and *Saxonian Landscape*. Edvard Munch, *Bathing Man*.
1919	Communist Revolt in Berlin. Paris Peace Conference adopts principle to found League of Nations. Benito Mussolini founds Fascist movement in Italy. Peace Treaty of Versailles signed. Britain and France authorise resumption of commercial relations with Germany. British-Persian agreement at Tehran to preserve integrity of Persia. Irish War of Independence begins. US Senate vetoes ratification of Versailles Treaty leaving US outside League of Nations.	Bauhaus movement founded by Walter Gropius. Wassily Kandinsky, *Dreamy Improvisation*. Paul Klee, *Dream Birds*. Thomas Hardy, *Collected Poems*. Herman Hesse, *Demian*. George Bernard Shaw, *Heartbreak House*. Edward Elgar, *Concerto in E Minor for Cello*. Film: *The Cabinet of Dr Caligari*.

YEAR	AGE	THE LIFE AND THE LAND
1920	56	Treaty of Trianon between Allies and Hungary: awards Romania most of territory Brătianu sought.
		Treaty of Union of Romania and Bessarabia: confirms Romania's sovereignty over province.
1922	58	Brătianu becomes Prime Minister of Liberal government that will remain in office for four years.

YEAR	HISTORY	CULTURE
1920	League of Nations comes into existence.	F Scott Fitzgerald, *This Side of Paradise*.
	The Hague selected as seat of International Court of Justice.	Franz Kafka, *The Country Doctor*.
	League of Nations headquarters moves to Geneva.	Katherine Mansfield, *Bliss*.
	Warren G Harding wins US Presidential election.	Rambert School of Ballet formed in London.
	Bolsheviks win Russian Civil War.	Lyonel Feininger, *Church*.
	Government of Ireland Act passed.	Juan Gris, *Book and Newspaper*. Vincent D'Indy, *The Legend Of St Christopher*.
	Adolf Hitler announces his 25-point programme in Munich.	Maurice Ravel, *La Valse*.
1922	Chanak crisis.	T S Eliot, *The Waste Land*.
	Britain recognises Kingdom of Egypt under Fuad I.	James Joyce, *Ulysses*. F Scott Fitzgerald, *The Beautiful and Damned*.
	Mahatma Gandhi sentenced to six years in prison for civil disobedience.	Hermann Hesse, *Siddartha*. Irving Berlin, *April Showers*.
	Election in Irish Free State gives majority to Pro-Treaty candidates: IRA takes large areas under its control.	British Broadcasting Company (later Corporation) (BBC) founded: first radio broadcasts.
	League of Nations Council approves British Mandate in Palestine.	Film: *Dr. Mabuse the Gambler*.

YEAR	AGE	THE LIFE AND THE LAND
1923	59	New constitution for Greater Romania reflecting Brătianu's ideas promulgated.
1925	61	Prince Carol, King Ferdinand's son and heir apparent, renounces rights to throne in favour of his four-year-old son Mihai.

YEAR	HISTORY	CULTURE
1923	French and Belgian troops occupy the Ruhr when Germany fails to make reparation payments. USSR formally comes into existence. Severe earthquake in Japan destroys all of Yokohama, most of Tokyo. Miguel Primo de Rivera assumes dictatorship of Spain. Wilhelm Marx succeeds Gustav Stresemann as German Chancellor. State of Emergency declared in Germany. British Mandate in Palestine begins. Adolf Hitler's *coup d'état* (Beer Hall Putsch) fails.	P G Wodehouse, *The Inimitable Jeeves.* Edna St Vincent Millay, *The Ballad of the Harp-Weaver; A Few Figs from Thistles.* Martin Buber, *I and Thou.* Sigmund Freud, *The Ego and the Id.* Max Beckmann, *The Trapeze.* Mark Chagall, *Love Idyll.* George Gershwin, *Rhapsody in Blue.* Bela Bartok, *Dance Suite.* BBC listings magazine *Radio Times* first published.
1925	Christiania, Norwegian capital, renamed Oslo. Mussolini announces he will take dictatorial powers in Italy. British Pound Sterling returns to Gold Standard. Paul von Hindenburg elected President of Germany. Hitler reorganises Nazi Party in Germany. Locarno Treaty signed in London.	Noel Coward, *Hay Fever.* Franz Kafka, *The Trial.* Virginia Woolf, *Mrs Dalloway.* Pablo Picasso, *Three Dancers.* Marc Chagall, *The Drinking Green Pig.* Ferruccio Busconi, *Doctor Faust.* Film: *Battleship Potemkin.*

YEAR	AGE	THE LIFE AND THE LAND
1926	62	Brătianu resigns as Prime Minister.
		Romania signs friendship treaty with France.

YEAR	HISTORY	CULTURE
1926	General Strike in Britain.	Franz Kafka, *The Castle*.
	Germany applies for admission to League of Nations; blocked by Spain and Brazil.	A A Milne, *Winnie the Pooh*.
		Ernest Hemingway, *The Sun Also Rises*.
	France proclaims the Lebanon republic.	Sean O'Casey, *The Plough and The Stars*.
	Germany admitted to League of Nations; Spain leaves as result.	Oskar Kokoschka, *Terrace in Richmond*.
	Imperial Conference in London decides Britain and Dominions are autonomous communities, equal in status.	Edvard Munch, *The Red House*.
		Eugene D'Albert, *The Golem*.
		Giacomo Puccini, *Turandot*.
	Leon Trotsky and Grigory Zinoviev expelled from Politburo of Communist Party following Stalin's victory in USSR.	Film: *The General*.

YEAR	AGE	THE LIFE AND THE LAND
1927	63	Brătianu returns as head of Liberal government.
		King Ferdinand dies, succeeded by his grandson Mihai, reigns under regency council.
		Brătianu dies at home in Bucharest.
1930		Prince Carol returns to Romania; two days later recognised as King by Parliament; Mihai becomes Crown Prince.

YEAR	HISTORY	CULTURE
1927	Inter-Allied military control of Germany ends.	Marcel Proust, *Le Temps Retrouvé.*
	'Black Friday' in Germany: economic system collapses.	Virginia Woolf, *To the Lighthouse.*
	Britain recognises rule of Ibn Saud in the Hijaz.	Jean Cocteau, *Orphee* and *Oedipe-Roi.*
	President Paul von Hindenburg repudiates Germany's responsibility for First World War.	Hermann Hesse, *Steppenwolf.* Adolf Hitler, *Mein Kampf.* Martin Heidegger, *Sein und Zeit.*
	Leon Trotsky and Grigory Zinoviev ultimately expelled from Soviet Communist Party.	J S Bach, *The Art of the Fugue.* George Gershwin, *Funny Face.*
	India Commission under Sir John Simon established to review Montagu-Chelmsford Act.	Georges Bracque, *Glass and Fruit.* Edward Hopper, *Manhattan Bridge.*
	Britain recognises Iraq's independence, promises to support its League of Nations membership application.	Film: *The Jazz Singer.*
1930	Britain, France, Italy, Japan and US sign London Naval Treaty regulating naval expansion.	T S Eliot, *Ash Wednesday.* W H Auden, *Poems.*
	Nazi politician Wilhelm Frick becomes Minister in Thuringia.	Noel Coward, *Private Lives.* Max Beckmann, *Self-portrait with a Saxophone.*
	German Nazi Party gains 107 seats.	Bela Bartok, *Cantata Profana.* Igor Stravinsky, *Symphony of Psalms.*
	Constantinople's name changed to Istanbul.	Alfred Adler, *The inferiority complex.*
	British Imperial Conference held in London: Statute of Westminster approved.	E K Chambers, *William Shakespeare.*
	Acrylic plastics invented.	Film: *All Quiet on the Western Front.*

YEAR	AGE	THE LIFE AND THE LAND
1933–7		Liberal Party in power; presses forward with neo-liberal economic agenda.
1938		King Carol II abolishes Constitution of 1923 in favour of one granting King full powers to rule; dissolves all political parties and groupings.

YEAR	HISTORY	CULTURE
1933–7	1933: Adolf Hitler appointed Chancellor of Germany.	1933: George Orwell, *Down and Out in Paris and London*.
	1934: USSR admitted to League of Nations.	1934: F Scott Fitzgerald, *Tender Is the Night*.
	1935: League of Nations imposes sanctions against Italy following invasion of Abyssinia.	1935: George Gershwin, *Porgy and Bess*.
	1936: German troops occupy Rhineland. Outbreak of Spanish Civil War.	1936: BBC begins world's first television transmission service.
	1937: Italy joins German–Japanese Anti-Comintern Pact.	1937: Film: *Snow White and the Seven Dwarfs*.
1938	German troops enter Austria declaring it part of German Reich.	J B Huizinga, *Homo Ludens*.
	Japanese puppet government of China at Nanjing.	Frank Lloyd Wright, Taliesen West, Phoenix, USA.
	Anti-Semitic legislation in Italy: no public employment or property.	Graham Greene, *Brighton Rock*.
	Munich Agreement hands Sudetenland to Germany.	Evelyn Waugh, *Scoop*.
	Kristallnacht in Germany: Jewish houses, synagogues and schools burnt for whole week.	Ballpoint pen patented in Hungary.
	US introduces minimum wage, age and maximum hours for employment.	*Picture Post* founded in Britain.
	Nuclear fission discovered in Germany.	Films: *Pygmalion. Alexander Nevsky. The Adventures of Robin Hood.*

YEAR	AGE	THE LIFE AND THE LAND
1940		Soviet Union demands 'return' of Bessarabia.
		Vienna Award imposed by Hitler requires Romania to cede North Transylvania to Hungary.
		King Carol II abdicates; succeeded by son Mihai I.
		Treaty of Craiova stipulates Romania's cession of southern Dobrudja to Bulgaria.
		Romania proclaimed National Legionary State: creation of new head of state Gen Ion Antonescu and Iron Guard.
		Antonescu signs Tripartite Pact: allies Romania with Germany, Italy and Japan.

YEAR	HISTORY	CULTURE
1940	Second World War:	Wassily Kandinsky, *Sky Blue*.
	Norwegian campaign failure causes Neville Chamberlain to resign: Winston Churchill becomes Britain's Prime Minister.	Graham Greene, *The Power and the Glory*.
		Ernest Hemingway, *For Whom the Bell Tolls*.
	Germany invades Holland, Belgium, Luxembourg.	Eugene O'Neill, *Long Days Journey into Night*.
	Italy declares war on France and Britain.	Films: *The Great Dictator*. *Pinocchio*. *Rebecca*.
	Battle of Britain.	
	France divides into German-occupied north and Vichy south.	
	Franklin D Roosevelt re-elected US President for unprecedented third term.	
	British victories against Italians in Western Desert.	
	Hungary and Romania join Axis.	
	Italy invades Greece.	

YEAR	AGE	THE LIFE AND THE LAND
1941		Antonescu wins struggle for power with Iron Guard; institutes military dictatorship.
		Romania joins Germany in war against Soviet Union.
1944		Antonescu regime overthrown in coup led by King Mihai and Liberal and National Peasant leaders with participation of Socialists and Communists.
		Romania joins Allies against Axis.

YEAR	HISTORY	CULTURE
1941	Second World War:	Etienne Gilson, *God and Philosophy.*
	British troops evacuate Greece, Crete falls.	Bertold Brecht, *Mother Courage and Her Children.*
	Germany invades USSR.	Noel Coward, *Blithe Spirit.*
	Japanese troops occupy Indochina.	British communist paper, *The Daily Worker*, suppressed.
	Germans besiege Leningrad and Moscow.	Films: *Citizen Kane. Dumbo. The Maltese Falcon.*
	Soviets counter-attack at Moscow.	
	Japan attacks Pearl Harbor, invades the Philippines.	
	Germany and Italy declare war on US.	
	Atomic bomb development begins in USA.	
1944	Second World War: British, US forces in Italy liberate Rome.	Carl Jung, *Psychology and Religion.*
	D-Day landings in France.	Michael Tippett, *A Child of Our Time.*
	Claus von Stauffenberg's bomb at Rastenburg fails to kill Hitler.	T S Eliot, *Four Quartets.*
	Churchill visits Stalin in Moscow.	Terrence Rattigan, *The Winslow Boy.*
	Free French enter Paris.	Tennessee Williams, *The Glass Menagerie.*
	Franklin D Roosevelt wins unprecedented fourth term as US President.	Film: *Double Indemnity. Henry V. Meet Me in St Louis.*
	German counter-offensive in the Ardennes.	Radio: *Much-Binding-in-the Marsh.*

YEAR	AGE	THE LIFE AND THE LAND
1947		King Mihai I forced to abdicate by Romanian Communist Party and its Soviet patrons; Romanian People's Republic proclaimed.

YEAR	HISTORY	CULTURE
1947	Hungary reassigned its 1938 frontiers.	Edinburgh Festival is founded.
	Moscow Conference fails over problem of Germany.	Albert Camus, *The Plague*.
		Anne Frank, *The Diary of Anne Frank*.
	'Truman Doctrine' pledges to support 'free peoples resisting subjugation by armed minorities or outside pressures'.	Tennessee Williams, *A Streetcar Named Desire*.
	US Secretary of State George C Marshall calls for relief aid to Europe.	Le Corbusier, Unité d'Habitation Marseille, France.
	Indian Independence and Partition.	Films: *Monsieur Verdoux. Black Narcissus*.
	Indonesian independence movement rises against Dutch troops: UN Security Council calls for ceasefire.	
	Communists win Hungarian election.	
	New Japanese constitution renounces use of war.	

Further Reading

The following notes are meant to suggest works as starting-points for further investigation. Books in English receive special attention, but, as is evident, a serious study of Ionel Brătianu and the Romania of his time must rely on works in Romanian. The bibliography in Romanian on him is extensive, but surprisingly he has been the subject of scholarly monographs only in the last 20 years. There are three that cover his whole career. The most comprehensive is Anastasie Iordache's *Ion I. C. Brătianu* (Editura Albatros, Bucureşti: 1994). Ioan Scurtu's *Ion I. C. Brătianu: Activitatea politică* (Editura Museion, Bucureşti: 1992) is a succinct overview of Brătianu's career indicating significant trends and turning points. Ion Novăceanu, *Ion I. C. Brătianu şi opţiunia occidentală a României* (Editura Mesagerul, Cluj-Napoca: 1996), emphasises his policy of Europeanization.

Brătianu obviously occupies an important place in studies about political parties and the art of politics of his time. Henry L Roberts' *Rumania: Political Problems of an Agrarian State* (Yale University Press, New Haven: 1951) remains an authoritative account for the interwar decades. Ion Scurtu's biographies, *Carol I* (Editura Eniclopedică, Bucureşti: 2001) and *Ferdinand I* (Editura Eniclopedică, Bucureşti: 2001), place Brătianu the politician in broad context. Z Ornea's *Viaţa lui C. Stere*, 2 vols (Cartea Românească, Bucuresti: 1989–1991) does the same, but with a richness of detail that also reveals the human being. Analyses of Romanian liberalism elucidate many aspects of Brătianu's thought and ambitions. Of great value in tracing the evolution of liberalism in general and in providing background for his career is Apostol Stan's biography of his father, *Ion C. Brătianu. Un promotor al liberalismului în România* (Editura Globus, Bucureşti: 1993). The most comprehensive study of Romanian liberalism, from the early 19th century to the present, is Constantin Nica, *Liberalismul din România: teorie şi practică*, 4 vols (Editura Institutului de Ştiinţe Politice şi Relaţii Internaţionale, Bucureşti: 2005–2008). The third volume is most pertinent for the Brătianu era.

On Romania and the First World War a good general account is by Victor Atanasiu and others, *România în primul război mondial* (Editura Militară, Bucureşti: 1979), which covers political and economic questions as well as military campaigns. The most recent history of military operations is *România în anii primului război mondial*, 2 vols (Editura Militară, Bucureşti: 1987), which preserves the patriotic tone of earlier such histories. The essays in Glenn E Torrey, *Romania and World War I* (Center for Romanian Studies, Iaşi: 1998), provide an authoritative evaluation of Romania's participation in the War. His biography of the head of the French military mission to Romania, *Henri Mathias Berthelot: Soldier of France, Defender of Romania* (Center for Romanian Studies, Iaşi: 2001), offers new perspectives on Brătianu as a wartime leader.

On peace-making at the end of the War, Sherman David

Spector, *Romania at the Paris Peace Conference* (Bookman Associates, New York: 1962; reprinted, Center for Romanian Studies, Iaşi: 1995), focuses on Brătianu's strained relations with the Allies and is based mainly on Western sources. In *Acţiunea politică şi militară a României în 1919*, 2nd ed (Cartea Românească, Bucureşti: 1940), Gheorghe I Brătianu draws on family archives to explain his father's objectives at Paris. Lucian Leuştian, *România, Ungaria şi Tratatul de la Trianon, 1918–1920* (Polirom, Iaşi: 2002), offers an up-to-date analysis of Brătianu's diplomacy. Useful for background for Romania at Paris are Gheorghe Căzan and Şerban Rădulescu-Zoner, *România şi Tripla Alianţă, 1878–1914* (Editura Ştiinţifică şi Enciclopedică, Bucureşti: 1979), which describes the main directions of Romanian foreign policy, and Vasile Vesa, *România şi Franţa la începutul secolului al XX-lea, 1900–1916* (Editura Dacia, Cluj-Napoca: 1975) and Constantin Nuţu, *România în anii neutralităţii, 1914–1916* (Editura Ştiinţifică, Bucureşti: 1972).

On major economic and social problems of the Brătianu era, a useful starting-point is the comparative analysis by Bogdan Murgescu, *România şi Europa* (Poliron, Iaşi: 2010), which places a modernising Romania within a broad European context. A detailed analysis of modern Romania's economic development is provided by Victor Axenciuc, *Evoluţia economică a României. Cercetări statistico-istorice 1859–1947*, 3 vols (Editura Academiei Române, Bucureşti: 1992–2000). Gheorghe Buzatu, *O istorie a petrolului românesc* (Editura Eniclopedică, Bucureşti: 1998), investigates the relationship between the Romanian state and Western oil companies. Ioan Saizu, *Politica economică a României între 1922 şi 1928* (Editura Academiei R. S. România, Bucureşti: 1981), describes the economic goals and policies of the Liberals during Brătianu's final tenure as Prime Minister. Fundamental for understanding the character and role of the middle class are the critical analyses of Ştefan Zeletin, *Burghezia română: Origina şi rolul ei istoric* (Cultura Naţională, Bucureşti: 1925) and Mihail Manoilescu, *Rostul şi destinul burgheziei româneşti* (Cugetarea, Bucureşti: 1942), both of which are now classics. On the Jewish question, Carol Iancu, *Les Juifs en Roumanie 1866–1919: De l'exclusion à l'émancipation* (Éditions de l'Université de Provence, Aix-en-Provence: 1978), offers well-documented guidance. On the Romanian question in Hungary one may consult Keith Hitchins, *A Nation Affirmed: The Romanian National Movement in Transylvania, 1860–1914* (Encyclopaedic Publishing House, Bucharest: 1999).

On cultural and intellectual life Z Ornea, *Tradiţionalism şi modernitate în deceniul al treilea* (Editura Eminescu, Bucureşti: 1980), is a thorough, balanced evaluation of significant trends and major figures of the 1930s. Of the many works on Romania between East and West, Mac Linscott Ricketts, *Mircea Eliade: The Romanian Roots, 1907–1945*, 2 vols. (East European Monographs, Boulder, Colorado: 1988), examines the intellectual effervescence of the time from the perspective of the leader of the young generation. In a classic work George Călinescu, *History of Romanian Literature* (UNESCO, Paris; Nagard, Milan: 1998), describes the Europeanization of Romanian prose and poetry and the persistence of nativist trends. Essays in Keith Hitchins, *The Identity of Romania*, 2nd ed (Encyclopaedic Publishing House, Bucharest: 2009), examine the debate among intellectuals on the character and destiny of the Romanians.

More general works on Romania help to place Brătianu and his times in a broad historical framework. The Romanian historian Lucian Boia has stirred controversy with his resolute questioning of Romanian historiographical orthodoxy in *History and Myth in Romanian Consciousness* (Central European University Press, Budapest: 2001). His *Romania: Borderland of Europe* (Reaktion Books, London: 2001) examines major issues of Romanian history in the same critical spirit. A comprehensive survey of the evolution of modern Romania is available in Keith Hitchins, *The Romanians, 1774–1866* (Clarendon Press, Oxford: 1996) and *Rumania, 1866–1947* (Clarendon Press, Oxford: 1994).

Picture Sources

The author and publishers wish to express their thanks to the following sources of illustrative material and/or permission to reproduce it. They will make proper acknowledgements in future editions in the event that any omissions have occurred.

Topham Picturepoint.

Endpapers

The Signing of Peace in the Hall of Mirrors, Versailles, 28th June 1919 by Sir William Orpen (Imperial War Museum: akg-images)
Front row: Dr Johannes Bell (Germany) signing with Herr Hermann Müller leaning over him
Middle row (seated, left to right): General Tasker H Bliss, Col E M House, Mr Henry White, Mr Robert Lansing, President Woodrow Wilson (United States); M Georges Clemenceau (France); Mr David Lloyd George, Mr Andrew Bonar Law, Mr Arthur J Balfour, Viscount Milner, Mr G N Barnes (Great Britain); Prince Saionji (Japan)
Back row (left to right): M Eleftherios Venizelos (Greece); Dr Afonso Costa (Portugal); Lord Riddell (British Press);

Sir George E Foster (Canada); M Nikola Pašić (Serbia); M Stephen Pichon (France); Col Sir Maurice Hankey, Mr Edwin S Montagu (Great Britain); the Maharajah of Bikaner (India); Signor Vittorio Emanuele Orlando (Italy); M Paul Hymans (Belgium); General Louis Botha (South Africa); Mr W M Hughes (Australia)

Jacket images

(Front): Imperial War Museum: akg Images.
(Back): *Peace Conference at the Quai d'Orsay* by Sir William Orpen (Imperial War Museum: akg Images).
Left to right (seated): Signor Orlando (Italy); Mr Robert Lansing, President Woodrow Wilson (United States); M Georges Clemenceau (France); Mr David Lloyd George, Mr Andrew Bonar Law, Mr Arthur J Balfour (Great Britain); Left to right (standing): M Paul Hymans (Belgium); Mr Eleftherios Venizelos (Greece); The Emir Feisal (The Hashemite Kingdom); Mr W F Massey (New Zealand); General Jan Smuts (South Africa); Col E M House (United States); General Louis Botha (South Africa); Prince Saionji (Japan); Mr W M Hughes (Australia); Sir Robert Borden (Canada); Mr G N Barnes (Great Britain); M Ignacy Paderewski (Poland)

Index

NB All family relationships are to Ionel Brătianu unless otherwise stated.

A

Adrianople, Treaty of 5
Aehrenthal, Graf Alois Lexa von 52–4
Alecsandri, Vasile 12
Alfred, Duke of Edinburgh 26
Antonescu, General Ion 156–7
Antonescu, Victor 107
Astor, Paulina 26
Aurelian, Petre S 31
Austria-Hungary 10, 49–53, 55–61, 63–73, 75–9, 83–4, 101, 102
Averescu, General Alexandru 32, 85–6, 94, 100, 127, 131, 134–5, 147–8

B

Balkan Wars, the 54–9
Banat, the 77, 79, 82, 83, 103, 107, 110, 117–19, 130, 132
Barclay, Sir George 97
Bataillard, Paul 7, 12
Belgium 15
Berchtold, Graf Leopold von 55–7, 59
Berthelot, General Henri 87, 93, 98, 99, 102
Bessarabia 10, 70, 79, 96, 101, 107, 110, 118, 130–1, 137, 146–7, 156
Bethmann-Hollweg, Theobald von 52–4
Blanc, Louis 7

Blondel, Camille 76, 77
Brătianu, Costandin
    (grandfather) 4
Brătianu, Dinu (brother) 17
Brătianu, Gheorghe (son)
    25–6
Brătianu, Iane (great-
    grandfather) 4
Brătianu, Ion C (father) 4,
    6, 8–10, 11, 14, 19, 43, 49
Brătianu, Ionel
    death 148
    education 6–7, 10–13
    engineering career 13–15
    family origins 3–4
    First World War, and the
        80–103
    Great Peasant Uprising,
        and the 31–3
    'Greater Romania', and
        48–64, 66, 130–2,
        133–48
    'Jewish Question', and
        the 44–7, 126, 139–40
    'Liberal Manifesto', the 42
    Liberal Party, and the
        18–19, 22–5
    Minorities Treaty, and
        the 116, 124–7
    modernisation of
        Romania, and the
        22–4, 27–44, 47, 141–3
    neutrality, and 67–79
    'Neo-Liberalism', and
        41–2
    Paris Peace Conference,
        at the 107–27
    separate peace with the
        Central Powers, and
        the 97–103
    Triple Alliance, and the
        49–58
Brătianu, Sabina (sister) 12
Brătianu, Vintilă (brother)
    86, 89, 153
Brest-Litovsk, Treaty of 98,
    100
Bucharest, Treaty of (1913)
    59, 63, 64, 66, 130
Buftea-Bucharest, Treaty of
    (1918) 100–1, 108, 111
Bukovina 66, 70, 77, 79, 82,
    102, 107, 110, 118, 137,
    156
Bulgaria 51, 53–9, 64, 66–7,
    69–70, 77, 83, 84, 85, 87,
    102, 108, 130, 130, 144, 156

C
Carada, Eugeniu 14, 17, 18
Caragiale, Ion Luca 38
Carol I of Romania, King
    9, 20, 32, 37, 44, 49–51,
    55–7, 58, 60, 63–8

Carol II of Romania, King
147–8, 154–8
Carp, Petre 35, 43, 63, 67,
81, 82
Chicherin, Georgy 146
Clemenceau, Georges 45,
98, 100, 119, 125–6
and Ionel Brătianu
108–9, 114–15, 117
Coandă, Constantin 102–3,
107, 129
Codreanu, Corneliu Zelea
155
Conrad von Hotzendorf,
Graf Franz 55–6, 66
Conservative Party 15, 19,
21, 23, 27, 31, 35, 39,
43–5, 50, 54–7, 60, 61,
63, 65, 71, 72, 92, 100,
134, 137, 139
Crimean War, the 8, 10, 40
Cuza, Prince Alexandru 6,
8, 25
Czechoslovakia 116, 146
Czernin, Graf Ottokar 60,
62, 66, 68, 74, 80

D
Democratic-Conservative
Party 21, 23, 41
Diamandy, Constantin
69–70, 75, 107

Dobrescu-Argeş,
Constantin 21
Duca, Ion G 82–3, 89, 153

F
Falkenhayn, General Erich
von 86, 88
Fasciotti, Baron Carlo 76
Ferdinand of Romania,
King 68, 72, 81, 103, 111,
134–5, 148
Filipescu, Nicolae 72
First World War, the 68–79,
80–103
France 8, 15, 51, 60, 63, 64,
69, 73, 75–9, 84, 93, 114,
144–5
Franchet d'Esperey, General
120, 123
Franz Ferdinand, Archduke
62, 64, 65

G
George V, King 114, 115
Germany 9, 10, 40, 49–50,
51–3, 64, 67–8, 73, 76,
83, 84, 90, 102, 146, 155,
156
Ghica, Ion 12
Great Britain 8, 51, 60, 69,
73–6, 78, 79, 114, 144,
145, 155

Greece 54, 57, 70, 116
Guchkov, Alexander 91–2

H
Hitler, Adolf 155–6
Hohenzollern-Sigmaringen,
    Prince Karl von *see* Carol
    of Romania, King
Hungary
    Romanian invasion of
        111, 119–21, 128–9, 130

I
Ionescu, Take 21, 23, 41, 72,
    89, 98, 99, 127
Iorga, Nicolae 30, 137
Iron Guard, the 83, 153, 155
Italy 10, 40, 45, 49, 68, 74, 76,
    77, 79, 89, 108, 119, 154

J
Japan 108
'Jewish Question, the 44–7,
    124–6
Junimea (Youth) Society of
    Iaşi, the 29, 30, 43

K
Károlyi, Mihály 120, 123
Kerensky, Alexander 91
Kogălniceanu, Mihail 6
Kornilov, General Lavr 94

Kun, Béla 110, 120–3, 128

L
Lavisse, Ernest 13
League of Nations, the 110,
    125, 146
League of the People, the
    127
Liberal Party 5, 10, 14, 15,
    17, 18–19, 22, 24–6, 36,
    37, 41–5, 47, 50, 51, 55,
    56, 57, 59, 60–1, 66, 72,
    92–3, 98, 99, 100–3, 125,
    127, 129, 133–9, 142–3,
    147–8, 153–4
Lisle, Lecomte de 13
Little Entente, the 23, 83,
    146
Lloyd George, David 45,
    100, 108, 115, 119, 144
    and Ionel Brătianu
        109–10, 121
Locarno Pact, the 146
London, Treaty of (1913) 57
London, Treaty of (1915) 76
Luzzatti, Luigi 45–6, 124

M
Macedonski, Alexandru 39
Mackensen, Field Marshal
    August von 84, 85, 94,
    98, 99

Maiorescu, Titu 29–30, 44, 57, 63, 72, 81
Maniu, Iuliu 61, 139
Marghiloman, Alexandru 27, 44, 72, 81–2, 100–2
Marie of Romania, Queen 26–7, 65
    Paris Peace Conference, at the 114–15
Michelet, Jules 7
Mickiewicz, Adam 7
Mihai, Prince 148, 156–7
Mihalache, Ion 139
Minorities Treaty, the 47, 109, 110–11, 116, 118, 124–9, 134, 139–41
Mişu, Nicolae 107
Moldavia 3, 4, 5, 6, 16, 41, 46, 70, 86, 90–2, 94–8, 101, 103, 142
Montenegro 54
Moruzi, Maria (1st wife) 25–6

N
National Peasant Party, the 139
Neuilly, Treaty of 130
Nicholas II, Tsar 64, 87, 114

O
Odobescu, Alexandru 12

Occult, the 14, 18, 37
Orlando, Vittorio 119
Ottoman Empire, the *see* Turkey

P
Paris Peace Conference, the 107–31
    Romanian delegation 107
Party of Labour, the 92–3
Peasant Committee, the 21–2
Peasant Party, the (1895–1905) 22
Peasant Party, the (founded 1905) 22, 93, 134, 139
Poland 116
Porumbacu, Emanoil 68

Q
Quinet, Edgar 7

R
Romania
    Austria-Hungary, and 49–51, 52–7, 59–64, 65–8, 83
    Balkan Wars, and the 54–9
    economy 10, 15–16, 22–3, 28–36, 42–4, 72–4, 84, 135–7, 141–3, 153–4

First World War, and the
  65–79, 80–103
France, and 6–8, 63–4,
  75, 76–9, 86–7, 90–1,
  97–8, 100, 109–10,
  144–5
Germany, and 10, 49–50,
  52–4, 67–8, 73,
  98–103, 154–6
Great Britain, and 51,
  97–8, 109–10, 145
Great Peasant Uprising
  (1907) 31–3
Hungary, invasion of
  111, 119–21, 128–9,
  130
'Jewish Question', the,
  and minorities 44–7,
  109, 110–11, 116, 118,
  124–9, 134, 139–41
neutrality (1914–16)
  65–79
'Oil Treaty', the 155
Paris Peace Conference
  delegation 107
Phanariot regime 4, 5
reparations, and 144
Russia, and 5, 7–8, 9–10,
  63–4, 65, 69–71, 75,
  77–9, 87, 90–2, 95–7,
  98–9, 131, 139, 144,
  146–7

Russo-Turkish War, and
  the 9–10
Second World War, and
  the 155–6
separate peace with the
  Central Powers, and
  the 97–103
Soviet occupation
  156–7
Triple Alliance, and the
  10, 49, 50–1, 55, 57,
  59–60, 62, 64, 66, 68
War for Independence,
  the 9–10
Romanian Communist
  Party, the 139, 157
Romanian National Party,
  the 60–2, 129, 133, 134,
  139
Russia 5, 7–8, 9–10, 49, 51,
  54, 60, 63–4, 65, 69–71,
  75, 76–9, 80, 81, 82, 84,
  87, 90–1, 108, 121, 130,
  131, 138, 139, 142, 144
  1917 Revolutions 91–2,
  95–9, 100, 101
Russo-Turkish War (1877)
  9–10

S
Saint-Aulaire, Count
  Charles 97

Saligny, Anghel 14, 16
Sămănătorists, the (Sowers)
    30
Sazonov, Sergey 63, 69–70,
    75
Second World War, the
    155–7
Serbia 54, 55, 57, 59–60, 65,
    67, 70, 71, 84, 90, 108,
    116
Shcherbachev, General
    Dmitry 98
Smuts, General Jan
    Christian 121–2
Social Democratic Party of
    Romania, the 22, 25
Soviet Union *see* Russia
Sowers, the *see*
    Sămănătorists, the
St Germain, Treaty of 127
Ştirby, Elisa (2nd wife) 25,
    27
Sturdza, Dimitrie A 14, 17,
    24–5, 37, 51

T
Tisza, István 61, 62, 63, 74
Transylvania 6, 49, 50, 53,
    59–64, 66–7, 72, 74, 77,
    79, 83, 85–9, 103, 107,

110, 118–20, 122, 128,
    129, 130, 132, 133, 137,
    139, 140, 141, 146, 156
Trianon, Treaty of 130
Triple Alliance, the 10, 49,
    50–1, 55, 57, 59–60, 62,
    64, 66, 68
Turkey 5, 7–8, 9–10, 33, 51,
    54, 56, 58, 70, 73, 83, 89,
    102

V
Vaida, Alexandru 129, 131,
    134
Văitoianu, General Arthur
    127–9
Versailles, Treaty of 127
Vlădescu, Şerban 4

W
Waldburg, Graf von 63
Wilson, Woodrow 108, 119
    and Ionel Brătianu
        110–11, 115–16, 122,
        126–7
Yugoslavia 130, 146

Z
Zamfirescu, Duiliu 38

Makers of the Modern World

UK PUBLICATION: November 2008 to December 2010
CLASSIFICATION: Biography/History/
 International Relations
FORMAT: 198 × 128mm
EXTENT: 208pp
ILLUSTRATIONS: 6 photographs plus 4 maps
TERRITORY: world

Chronology of life in context, full index, bibliography innovative layout with sidebars

Woodrow Wilson: United States of America by Brian Morton
Friedrich Ebert: Germany by Harry Harmer
Georges Clemenceau: France by David Watson
David Lloyd George: Great Britain by Alan Sharp
Prince Saionji: Japan by Jonathan Clements
Wellington Koo: China by Jonathan Clements
Eleftherios Venizelos: Greece by Andrew Dalby
From the Sultan to Atatürk: Turkey by Andrew Mango
The Hashemites: The Dream of Arabia by Robert McNamara
Chaim Weizmann: The Dream of Zion by Tom Fraser
Piip, Meierovics & Voldemaras: Estonia, Latvia & Lithuania by Charlotte Alston
Ignacy Paderewski: Poland by Anita Prazmowska
Beneš, Masaryk: Czechoslovakia by Peter Neville
Károlyi & Bethlen: Hungary by Bryan Cartledge
Karl Renner: Austria by Jamie Bulloch
Vittorio Orlando: Italy by Spencer Di Scala
Pašić & Trumbić: The Kingdom of Serbs, Croats and Slovenes by Dejan Djokic
Aleksandŭr Stamboliĭski: Bulgaria by R J Crampton
Ion Bratianu: Romania by Keith Hitchin
Paul Hymans: Belgium by Sally Marks
General Smuts: South Africa by Antony Lentin
William Hughes: Australia by Carl Bridge
William Massey: New Zealand by James Watson
Sir Robert Borden: Canada by Martin Thornton
Maharajah of Bikaner: India by Hugh Purcell
Afonso Costa: Portugal by Filipe Ribeiro de Meneses
Epitácio Pessoa: Brazil by Michael Streeter
South America by Michael Streeter
Central America by Michael Streeter
South East Asia by Andrew Dalby
The League of Nations by Ruth Henig
Consequences of Peace: The Versailles Settlement – Aftermath and Legacy
 by Alan Sharp